Succeeding
at
Teaching
Mathematics
K–6

The authors wish to dedicate this book to their husbands, Eric and Eric.

Succeeding
at
Teaching
Mathematics
K–6

Julie Sliva Spitzer // Cheryl D. Roddick

CORWIN PRESS
A SAGE Company
Thousand Oaks, CA 91320

For information:

Corwin Press
A SAGE Company
2455 Teller Road
Thousand Oaks, California 91320
www.corwinpress.com

SAGE Ltd.
1 Oliver's Yard
55 City Road
London EC1Y 1SP
United Kingdom

SAGE India Pvt. Ltd.
B 1/I 1 Mohan
  Cooperative Industrial Area
Mathura Road, New Delhi 110 044
India

SAGE Asia-Pacific Pte. Ltd.
33 Pekin Street #02-01
Far East Square
Singapore 048763

Library of Congress Cataloging-in-Publication Data

Spitzer, Julie Sliva.
Succeeding at teaching mathematics, K–6/by Julie Sliva Spitzer and Cheryl D. Roddick.
    p. cm.
Includes bibliographical references and index.
ISBN 978-1-4129-2764-2 (cloth)
ISBN 978-1-4129-2765-9 (pbk.)
    1. Mathematics—Study and teaching (Elementary) I. Roddick, Cheryl D. II. Title.

QA135.6.S65 2008
372.7—dc22   2007020445

This book is printed on acid-free paper.

07   08   09   10   11   10 9 8 7 6 5 4 3 2 1

Acquisitions Editor:	Kylee Liegl
Managing Editor:	David Chao
Editorial Assistant:	Mary Dang
Production Editor:	Cassandra Margaret Seibel
Copy Editor:	Marilyn Power Scott
Typesetter:	C&M Digitals (P) Ltd.
Proofreader:	Anne Rogers
Indexer:	Gloria Tierney
Cover Designer:	Rose Storey
Graphic Designer:	Karine Hovsepian

Contents

Acknowledgments

The authors would like to thank all of those people who have assisted us in producing this book: Allyson Sharp, Mary Dang, Marilyn Power Scott, and Jean Ward. We also would like to thank the reviewers who gave us many thoughtful comments on earlier versions of the book:

Coleen Martin
Fifth Grade Teacher
Dunlap District #323
Wilder Waite Grade School
Peoria, IL

Carolynn Montgomery
Fourth Grade Inclusion Teacher
John Baker Elementary School
Albuquerque, NM

Sharon Young
Professor, Mathematics Education
Department of Mathematics
Seattle Pacific University
Seattle, WA

About the Authors

 **Julie Sliva Spitzer** is an associate professor in the Department of Mathematics at San José State University. She currently teaches mathematics and mathematics methods courses to aspiring K–12 educators in addition to supervising field experiences for student teachers at the secondary level. She continues to enjoy inservice activities with teachers of Grades K–12.

Dr. Spitzer's research interests include studying teacher and student attitudes toward teaching and learning mathematics and best practices for teaching mathematics to special needs learners. In addition, Dr. Spitzer is a frequent presenter at the National Council of Teachers of Mathematics Annual Conference, the California Mathematics Council–Northern Section Annual Conference, and the Psychology of Mathematics Education, North American Chapter Conference. Dr. Spitzer can be reached at sliva@math.sjsu.edu.

 **Cheryl D. Roddick** is an associate professor in the Department of Mathematics at San José State University. She currently teaches mathematics and mathematics methods courses to students in K–12 education. She also supervises field experiences for student teachers at the secondary level.

Dr. Roddick's research interests include the conceptual understanding of fractions and teacher change relative to teaching mathematics. She has presented her research in local as well as national mathematics education conferences. She also facilitates K–12 inservice activities with teachers in local school districts. Dr. Roddick may be reached at roddick@math.sjsu.edu.

Introduction

Over our collective years as mathematics educators, we have found that new teachers kept asking us the same questions over and over. The crucial one has been, "How can I be the most effective teacher for my students?" We realized that there is a critical need for more information on this topic to be made available for new mathematics teachers, to make their transition to teaching mathematics easier. That is our goal with this book.

In it, we have used a combination of research, personal experiences, and observations of other mathematics teachers. We have included many of the common problems and big ideas in mathematics in many vignettes sprinkled throughout the book. Most of the vignettes were inspired by real teachers in real classrooms, and we hope they encourage thought-provoking discussion on important issues in content as well as pedagogy in K–6 mathematics lessons.

We would like you to keep in mind as you read this book that there is no one right way to approach teaching. And now is the time for you to develop your own philosophy of teaching and learning. Before you begin reading, please picture your ideal class: What will the students be doing? What will you be doing? We believe you must start with a vision of what you desire for your career and your students. It is our hope that this book will help you to get there. It is meant to be used as a tool to help you think about the important issues that will shape the kind of teacher you are meant to be.

HOW THE BOOK IS ORGANIZED

Chapter 1: "A Glimpse at Mathematics Instruction." This chapter provides a look at mathematics instruction in two elementary classrooms. With two vignettes we set the stage for the rest of the book by introducing elements of successful mathematics instruction.

Chapter 2: "Standards-Based Teaching." In this chapter we build on the elements of successful mathematics instruction from Chapter 1 by discussing standards-based teaching in mathematics. We look at the standards set forth by the National Council of Teachers of Mathematics, as well as discuss the importance of standards created at the state and district levels. We also provide examples of standards-based teaching at different grade levels.

Chapter 3: "Engaging Students in Learning Mathematics." In this chapter we take a look at the three interrelated components of engagement: affective, behavioral, and cognitive. We begin with the affective component in light of Glasser's categorization of a human being's Five Basic Needs: (1) survival, (2) love and belonging, (3) fun, (4) freedom, and (5) power. We describe how each of these basic needs is reflected in the classroom and how you can use knowledge of these basic needs to create an inclusive classroom environment.

Chapter 4: "Engagement Strategies for Special Populations." This section of the book takes an in-depth view of strategies for engaging several special populations: special-needs students, gifted students, and English language learners. We discuss strategies for engagement that are specific to these special populations. We then present an engaging activity involving tessellations and discuss how this activity may engage special populations of students.

Chapter 5: "Assessment." This book would be incomplete if it did not address assessment and its importance in the instructional process. We address assessment by looking at the purposes of assessment and the backward design model for assessment. We also discuss different means of assessing mathematical understanding and give examples of each. We demonstrate how to change a multiple-choice question into each of the types of assessments discussed in this section. We also present suggestions for assessing special needs students.

Chapter 6: "Putting It All Together." In this last chapter, we discuss ways for you to incorporate the elements of this book throughout your mathematics curriculum. We suggest ways to connect big ideas within mathematics as well as present ideas for you to connect mathematics with other subjects.

Appendices. There are three appendices containing useful information at the end of the book. In Appendix A, we discuss ways you can communicate with your students' families. In Appendix B, we list books and other resources that connect mathematics and literature. In Appendix C, we highlight the importance of your development as a teacher of mathematics.

Your first years teaching are a very exciting time, and we hope that this book will provide you with a structure to plan and guide you through your teaching. We wish you the very best for a long, rewarding career doing what we believe is the best job anyone can have.

1

A Glimpse at Mathematics Instruction

It is your first day of school. You have spent quite a bit of time planning for this day, and you are ready. As you open your door, you see children and their parents approaching you. You feel a bit nervous, but the nervousness quickly transforms into excitement as you smile and welcome each of the new faces into your classroom. They smile back at you, and you know immediately that it is going to be a great year.

Is this the dream you have about your first day of teaching? Do you imagine that everything will fall into place as a result of your hard work and preparation? Or is your rendition a little less than the ideal described above? Do you feel so unprepared for your teaching career that you don't even know where to turn for help? Whether you are at one extreme or the other, or somewhere in between, this book can help you prepare for the many aspects of teaching mathematics so that you will be able to make informed decisions on what to teach as well as how to teach it.

TWO ILLUSTRATIONS

Let's begin by looking at two elementary mathematics classrooms. One is a second grade lesson on subtraction; the other a fourth grade lesson on fractions. Both teachers are experienced and demonstrate many exemplary

practices in the teaching of mathematics. As you read, see if you can identify these teaching practices. At the end of each narrative, we discuss them.

Vignette 1: Second Grade—Subtraction With Regrouping

Miss Barilla is ready to introduce the concept of subtraction with regrouping. Prior to this lesson she has spent a good deal of time on addition and has introduced sub-traction. On the basis of her students' feedback, she is comfortable about moving on to subtraction with regrouping, and she has several main goals for today's les-son. The first is to provide her students with a deep understanding of subtraction through a variety of different types of problems. In her experience, she has found that the prevailing model for subtraction is the take-away model. However, she has planned to present problems that involve other models, such as comparing two quantities, separating a set into two disjoint sets, and finding the missing addend. She believes that in presenting a variety of problem situations she will prepare her students to become more flexible problem solvers. Over the course of the subtrac-tion unit she will provide many examples of the different types.

Miss Barilla's second goal is for her students to develop their own ways to approach problems that can be solved using subtraction. Her third goal is to intro-duce her students to the concept of regrouping during subtraction. The mathemat-ics text she uses has pictures of the base-ten blocks, but many of her colleagues have told her not to use the blocks with the students. They believe that manipulatives such as base-ten blocks are useful but take up too much class time. She realizes, however, that students have different learning styles, and she has learned to approach con-cepts in a hands-on manner initially and then progress to a more abstract manner. So she is providing each student with base-ten blocks so that they have a concrete method to begin with.

In addition to the mathematics content goals, she has been working on her students' abilities to communicate mathematically. Although her students are only in second grade, she wants them to begin to discuss their ideas, both with their class-mates in small groups and in whole-class instruction. She will also ask students to explain their solution methods to the class so that the group can see the different approaches of their classmates. This is a deliberate inclusion in her lesson plan, as she believes this will make her students better problem solvers by having more exposure to alternative solutions.

Miss Barilla has also been working on encouraging a positive attitude in her students toward learning mathematics. Over the past few weeks she has been con-sciously praising her students for their efforts during the mathematics lessons. In addition, she has posted her students' best papers on a wall designated for mathe-matics. Every week, when she hangs up the new papers, students rush to the wall excitedly to see whose papers have been displayed. Miss Barilla has been careful not to post the same students' papers each week in order to give more students the chance to take pride in their work. She has noticed that as a result of these small efforts, her students have become more interested in their mathematics lessons and in trying harder to do well.

Miss Barilla circulates around the classroom as the students begin their mathematics lesson by working on a warm-up problem written on the board:

> Shana and Greg are both participating in a school reading contest. Shana has read 31 pages this year and Greg has read 27. How many more pages does Greg need to read to have read as many as Shana?

She includes a warm-up problem each day to help her students transition from other content areas to mathematics and to refresh prerequisite skills needed for the day's content. Students have been instructed to solve the warm-up problem using the base-ten blocks that have been provided. Their task is to show how they solved the problem, draw pictures of their solution approach, and write their answer. This is a problem that can be solved by addition and has been chosen so that Miss Barilla can begin to build the connection from addition to subtraction with regrouping.

The students quickly go to work. Because they know how to add using the base-ten blocks, most of the students start with 27 blocks and count up until they get to 31. One student is asked to explain her solution method, and she responds by using the addition strategy. Miss Barilla thanks her for her answer, and then asks the class if they could solve the problem another way, without using addition. After a few minutes of silence one student hesitantly says, "subtraction?" Miss Barilla tells the student he is on the right track and then reviews the base-ten block solution that was just given using addition. She shows how students can add blocks to 27 until they get 31, keeping track of what they added. She goes on to regroup by trading in 10 unit blocks for 1 tens stick, so that 31 is represented by 3 tens sticks and 1 unit block. She then refers back to her student who suggested subtraction and models the problem by starting with 31 blocks and trying to take away 27. "We cannot take away 27 from 31 without making a trade with our blocks." She carefully displays the process of trading 1 tens stick for 10 unit cubes on the overhead. The quantity 31 is now represented by 2 tens sticks and 11 unit blocks, and then she can simply take 2 tens sticks and 7 unit blocks away, to arrive at an answer of 4.

Miss Barilla then puts her students together in carefully selected pairs based on her knowledge of the students. Some of her students have special learning needs; some are English language learners, whereas other students are gifted. Although these pairs were designed to support all learners, they specifically encourage English language learners by allowing them to work with a trusted peer. This approach promotes an atmosphere of acceptance and helps to foster the comfort of all students in participating in instructional activities. Miss Barilla was careful to place one of her English language learners, Juan, with a patient student, Antonio, who could translate whenever Juan had difficulty understanding the task. This was working well for both students, as Juan seemed to increase his participation in the assignment. One of Miss Barilla's special needs students, Jacqueline, was placed with another student who was not overpowering in relation to her. At the end of the day, Miss Barilla will discreetly ask these students how comfortable they felt in their pairs.

Miss Barilla then passes out the following three problems to the students:

1. Miss Barilla brought 12 cupcakes to school, and 7 have already been eaten. How many cupcakes are left?

2. If we have 23 students in our class and 18 chairs, how many more chairs will we need so that all of the students will have a place to sit?

3. Miss Barilla's class collected 31 bags of food to donate for Thanksgiving, and Mr. Daquila's class collected 16 bags of food. How many more bags of food did Miss Barilla's class collect?

Miss Barilla asks her students to discuss their answers in pairs before they present them on the overhead projector. The students have similar directions as with the warm-up: They are to explain their thinking using the base-ten blocks. Their task is to show how they solved the problem, draw pictures of their solution approach, and then write their answer.

While the students are working on their problems, Miss Barilla visits each pair of students to observe and discuss their progress. The first problem about cupcakes is a take-away problem, and most students have modeled the problem accordingly. One pair demonstrates the problem using 12 unit blocks and then takes 7 of those unit blocks away. Miss Barilla praises the students and asks them whether they solved the third problem in the same way. "We had a hard time with that one, because the numbers are bigger," one student says. Another student expresses her frustration as well. "I thought we should solve it the same way as the first problem, but it doesn't work the same way." "Why is that?" Miss Barilla asks. "Well," began the second student, "in the first problem we took away 7 cupcakes because those were eaten. But in the third problem there is nothing to take away." (Note: This problem is a "comparison" problem and is not typically modeled in the same way as a take-away problem. The students realized this, thus the confusion.) "Right," chimes in the other student. "And we don't have enough blocks." Miss Barilla suggests to the students that they could replace the large numbers with the smaller numbers from the first problem and solve that simpler problem: She tells them they can use 12 instead of 31 and 7 instead of 16 (note that Miss Barilla has substituted the numbers from the first problem). They use the smaller numbers, but this time they create two groups to represent the two different classes' bags of food. They separate 7 blocks from the group of 12 and count the remaining blocks. Then they collectively agree that they can solve the initial problem. Miss Barilla encourages them to continue and moves on to other students.

This next pair has figured out that the larger numbers, such as 23, can be represented by using two tens sticks and three unit blocks instead of 23 unit blocks. Although this representation is quicker, it makes the subtraction harder because now they cannot subtract 18 from 23 without trading one of the tens sticks for 10 unit blocks. Miss Barilla is delighted that some of the groups have tried this on their own because this representation leads into the process of regrouping using the base-ten blocks. She watches this group as they work and hears one student say, "We cannot subtract 18 using these blocks." Miss Barilla asks, "Is there anything you have that you can trade to make it easier?" The students are silent for a moment until one of them points out that they can trade 1 tens stick for 10 unit blocks. Again, Miss Barilla stays with the students until they finish working the problem and she is convinced they are on the right path, then she moves on. To her surprise, the next pair has solved this problem as an addition problem, showing 18 blocks and counting how many they added to get to 23. Miss Barilla marvels at their response and makes a mental note to send this group to the board to show their alternative solution method.

While Miss Barilla checks on the progress of each pair of students, she is also mentally deciding which groups to send to the board based on the diversity and richness of their solutions and the clarity of their verbal explanations. Some of the problems are presented by more than one group because Miss Barilla wants the students to be exposed to a variety of solution methods and explanations, including the connection between addition and subtraction that was demonstrated in the second problem.

After all of the problems are explained at the board, Miss Barilla asks her students to verbalize what they have learned. Several students are called on, and Miss Barilla provides closure by summarizing these thoughts in her own words. The students are then instructed to each create a subtraction problem and ask a peer (their partner) to solve it. After they share their problems with their partners, they then share them with another pair. If the group of four finish early, they are asked to create a challenge problem for another group of four and to share it with another group.

The students have a short homework assignment, which follows. Miss Barilla wants to make sure that her students understand what is expected of them before they leave for the day. She hands out the following worksheet to each student as well as a small baggie with a set of paper base-ten blocks.

Solve the problems below and draw pictures to represent each of your answers. You may trace your base-ten blocks or draw your own.

1. Jack had 14 chocolates; his brother Dan ate 9 of them. How many chocolates does Jack have left?

Picture:

Number answer: Jack has _____ chocolates left.

2. Trisha has 15 oranges and Fred has 7. How many more oranges does Trisha have than Fred?

Picture:

Number answer: Trisha has ____ more oranges than Fred.

3. Together Tom and Tim shot 12 baskets at recess. If Tom shot 3 baskets, how many baskets did Tim shoot?

Picture:

Number answer: Tim shot ____ baskets.

As this 50-minute lesson ends, Miss Barilla reflects on the lesson. She mentally notes that many of the students had trouble using the manipulatives to represent the problem situation, and they needed help with regrouping once they were able to use both tens sticks and unit blocks. She also noticed that students wanted to solve all the problems as take-away problems. Although she prefers to allow her students to develop their own meaning to a problem instead of forcing a particular model on them, she realizes that she needs to continue to expose her students to different types of subtraction problems as well as different solution approaches. What occurred today will reshape what she has planned for the next few days of instruction.

Discussion

You probably noticed several important teaching practices in this vignette. You may have noticed that Miss Barilla has well-defined goals for her lesson and a clear development of the concepts involved. In this lesson she addresses one of the major content areas of second grade mathematics: subtraction. To encourage a rich understanding of subtraction, she has given students contexts that go beyond the classic take-away model. She also provides students with base-ten blocks to concretely develop the concept of regrouping and to give meaning to the subtraction algorithm, which will be introduced in a future lesson. Links to addition and subtraction were made explicit so as to illustrate the connections between these two operations. During the lesson, Miss Barilla allowed the students to determine a workable model and solution method for each of the problems, rather than explaining a so-called right way to do the problem. By using this approach, she encouraged each student to create his or her own understanding of the problems and to develop a conceptual understanding of subtraction.

Because students approached these problems collaboratively, communication played an important role in their understanding of the lesson. They were required to discuss their answers to the problems given to them as well as to write their own problems. All students had small-group interactions; in addition, some students explained their answers to the entire class. The students who finished their problems early had the opportunity to create more challenging problems within a small group. This allowed higher-achieving students to work on more complicated problems involving subtraction and to deepen their understanding by communicating with others.

This lesson was presented in a manner appropriate for second graders and encouraged active construction of understanding and participation by all. It allowed for all students to have access to addition and subtraction in some form, thus promoting a positive attitude toward learning mathematics. The teacher gave each student base-ten blocks to use as objects to physically manipulate, rather than just having the pictures of the blocks on a handout, or worse, only numbers on a page. She also asked students to use several different representations of subtraction and to make connections to other mathematical content (addition) and grouping in base ten.

Miss Barilla demonstrated that she has high expectations for all of her students by selecting content that is age appropriate and teaching it by building on the experiences and knowledge of her students. The students were engaged in activities that required them to be actively involved in their own learning. They were also encouraged for their efforts, which led to more positive attitudes toward mathematics. Miss Barilla also specifically made accommodations for her students with special needs so that they could fully participate in the learning activity. Although there was no formal assessment measure in the lesson, informal assessment was used throughout for instructional purposes. She used this information both to determine pace and direction in this lesson as well as for future, related lessons.

Vignette 2: Fourth Grade—Developing the Concept of Fractions

Students in Mr. Callahan's class have just gotten into their groups to start their investigation of the day. Mr. Callahan has spent a lot of time planning this lesson, because he knows from prior experience that the way he develops the concept of equivalent fractions is critical for their future understanding. During fifth and sixth grades, students generally spend a good deal of time learning the procedures for addition, subtraction, multiplication, and division of fractions. Mr. Callahan is a fourth grade teacher, and he knows he could teach these procedures by directly showing the students the necessary computations step by step and having them practice these steps by doing lots of similar problems. This is one way he has taught fractions in the past, and he used to think that this method was the best way to prepare his students for solving harder fraction problems in the fifth and sixth grades.

Yet over the years he has had many conversations with colleagues who teach fifth and sixth grade mathematics. Fractions are a big topic of concern, and the teachers feel that students have not developed an adequate conceptual understanding of equivalent fractions before proceeding to fraction arithmetic. It is precisely this understanding of equivalent fractions that is critical to the teaching and learning of addition and subtraction of fractions. Mr. Callahan has also spent some time comparing the fraction lessons in his text with the district requirements for teaching fractions in the fourth grade, as well as the National Council of Teachers of Mathematics standards for fractions in Grades 3–5, and he has discovered that it is not necessary to teach all of the material in the book to prepare his students for the fifth grade requirements. So in the past few years Mr. Callahan has taken a different approach, teaching fractions conceptually using a hands-on approach. He was pleased to learn that research supported his personal experiences using concrete manipulatives as a stepping stone to the abstract manipulations of numbers (e.g., Bley & Thornton, 2001).

The lesson for the day is about teaching equivalent fractions, one of the key concepts for fractions at this level. In previous lessons Mr. Callahan has allowed adequate time to introduce pattern blocks for working with fractions. He has encouraged the students to explore the relationships between the green equilateral triangle, blue rhombus, red isosceles trapezoid, and yellow hexagon. Students have been allowed to create their own sets of pattern blocks (useful for homework assignments) by cutting out their own pieces to use as a tool kit for learning fractions. Students have previously used different pattern block pieces to represent the whole and have determined fractional parts of a whole. In addition, students have learned the concept of fair trade, which is important when using pattern blocks to create equivalent fractions. For example, two green triangles are a fair trade for one blue rhombus, and two red trapezoids are a fair trade for one yellow hexagon. As he begins the lesson, Mr. Callahan is satisfied that students are at ease with using the pattern blocks to represent fractions.

Mr. Callahan begins the class by having students work in previously assigned pairs on the following warm-up problem:

> *Let the yellow hexagon = 1.*
>
> *1. Using pattern blocks, show two different ways to represent $^2/_3$.*
>
> *2. On your paper, draw or trace your pattern blocks and write the fraction that your picture represents.*
>
> *3. Why are both of these pictures equal to $^2/_3$? Explain your thinking.*

Mr. Callahan monitors student progress and notices that most students have only found one answer. He brings the class back together to go over their answers. He calls on a student to tell him one of her answers. She gives the answer of 2 blue rhombuses as a way to represent $^2/_3$. When asked how she knows this is correct, she replies, "I know that three blue rhombuses are a fair trade for one yellow hexagon. So that gives me thirds. To make two thirds, I just need two of these blue pieces." Another student is then called on to give his second answer. He tells Mr. Callahan that he could only find one answer, and murmurs among the class confirm that others had the same experience. "There is only one way to get thirds," another student offers.

At this point Mr. Callahan quickly sees that a majority of his students are having difficulty creating a second representation of $^2/_3$, and he needs to take this opportunity to revisit the concept of fair trade. This slightly alters what he has planned for the remainder of the lesson; however, he feels this concept is integral to their understanding of the concept of fractions and should be addressed.

He begins by discussing the idea of fair trade with money and pulls out a dollar from his pocket. "I have a dollar and I want to make a fair trade with you," he begins. "What are the different ways you can give me the equivalent amount using coins?" Many of the students raise their hands immediately, and he calls on several students to give him different fair trades for a dollar. Then he brings the conversation back to the pattern blocks and asks the following question: "You know that two blue rhombuses is one answer to the warm-up question. Are there any other fair trades that you can make?"

The students all busy themselves with their pattern blocks. A couple of students sitting next to each other discuss the problem quickly, then remind the class that two equilateral triangles is a fair trade for one blue rhombus, so four equilateral triangles must be another representation of $^2/_3$. But one of the students is not convinced. She says that four green triangles is really $^4/_6$ because it is four pieces out of six, not $^2/_3$. Mr. Callahan asks the students to consider what the student has said and whether *anyone has a response to her. At first, no one answers. Mr. Callahan asks, "Is there any way to determine whether or not four out of six green triangles is equivalent to two out of three blue rhombuses?"*

After several minutes of silence, one student points to his pattern blocks excitedly and says, "I know!" He shows the class how he has stacked four green triangles on top of the two blue rhombuses to cover the rhombuses exactly. "This proves that they are the same!" Mr. Callahan asks the student to show the whole class what he has just done using the overhead pattern blocks. After a few minutes of discussion, he feels the class is ready to proceed to the next activity.

Students are given the following problem:

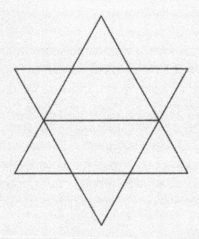

Choose one of the following fractions: $\frac{1}{2}$, $\frac{1}{3}$, $\frac{2}{3}$, $\frac{2}{4}$, $\frac{3}{4}$, $\frac{1}{6}$, $\frac{2}{6}$, $\frac{3}{12}$, and $\frac{8}{12}$. Using the given figure to represent one, find as many different ways to represent your fraction as you can, using pattern blocks. In addition, determine what other fractions your fraction is equivalent to (e.g., $\frac{1}{2}$ is equal to one yellow hexagon. It is also equal to two red trapezoids, which demonstrates that $\frac{1}{2}$ is equal to $\frac{2}{4}$).

The students quickly organize themselves into prearranged groups. Mr. Callahan has worked diligently to provide a structure for his students in which they can be most successful in their cooperative groups. He has spent time getting to know his students' strengths and weaknesses so that he can place them as effectively as possible in their groups. Overall, Mr. Callahan notes that students who appear more hesitant about their mathematical or language abilities tend to be less involved in the problem-solving process when they are placed with students who appear to be very confident in their abilities. As a result, since the beginning of the school year, he has created a structure for their cooperative group efforts; this includes roles and responsibilities for each student. The four roles are (1) leader (responsible for making sure each student in the group is heard from and focuses the learning around the task); (2) recorder (responsible for writing all of the group members' ideas down so everyone can see them); (3) time keeper/errand monitor (responsible for keeping track of time, getting materials that are needed, and obtaining help as needed from the teacher); and (4) presenter (presents the finished work to the entire class). Mr. Callahan has found he needs to explain the roles in detail and have students role play for clarity. In addition, he rotates the roles as well as members of the groups when needed.

As students work on their problem, Mr. Callahan walks around the room, listening in on each of the groups and helping where assistance is needed. As the students finish the task, he asks each group to place the solution to their problem on the board. Students are allowed to bring a group member for support when talking in front of the whole class.

After students have found the equivalent fractions, Mr. Callahan has them consider all the different representations of $1/2$. He writes them all on the board as follows:

$$\frac{1}{2} = \frac{2}{4} = \frac{3}{6} = \frac{6}{12}$$

and also this :

$$\frac{1}{2} = \frac{2}{4}; \quad \frac{1}{2} = \frac{3}{6}; \quad \frac{1}{2} = \frac{6}{12}$$

Up to this point, decisions about equality have been made by referring to the pattern blocks and determining whether a fair trade had been made. Now Mr. Callahan wants his students to see the numerical pattern used to create groups of equivalent fractions. "What patterns do you see in the fractions here?" he asks the class. He points to the problem on the board done by one of the groups. Students call out all sorts of interesting patterns, and one student points out that multiplying the numerator and denominator by the same value will always give you an equivalent fraction. Mr. Callahan doesn't elaborate on this idea today, because he plans to continue with the pattern blocks. He wants students to continue to deepen their understanding of what is meant by the numerators and denominators by referring to the relative size of the pattern blocks. He will revisit the numerical patterns later on and build on today's lesson in the future.

Mr. Callahan decides that the students have made sufficient progress and gives them the following problem to work on for homework:

Let one yellow hexagon represent one pizza. Divide this pizza evenly among six people.

1. What fraction does one person get?

2. If two people are sitting together, what fraction of the whole pizza do they get? (Remember that you are still sharing the pizza among six people.)

3. *Is the fraction in Question 2 equivalent to (the same as) any other fraction? If so, which fraction? (Hint: Think of a fair trade.)*

4. *What fraction of the whole pizza do three people sitting together get?*

5. *Is the fraction in Question 4 equivalent to any other fraction? If so, which fraction?*

6. *What fraction of the whole pizza do four people sitting together get?*

7. *Is the fraction in Question 6 equivalent to any other fraction? If so, which fraction?*

Students are asked to use their pattern blocks at home to solve this problem and to draw pictures of their solutions as well as write out the fractions. Mr. Callahan allows his students to begin working on this problem before the end of class so that he can check their understanding.

At the end of the day, Mr. Callahan reflects on the lesson. He thought the students would understand the idea of fair trade and that he would be able to move through the activities more quickly than he did. He was a bit puzzled, but then he remembered that the concept of equivalent fractions is a key concept at this grade level, and he needs to provide a sufficient amount of time for that idea to develop. He plans to spend a few more days with the pattern blocks, giving his students problems similar to the ones they did today. He has made a mental note to include a journal assignment about the concept of equivalent fractions (see p. 79, Chapter 5, for details on the journal assignment.) He will also assign some word problems involving addition and subtraction of fractions but will not teach the procedure for solving the problems by finding common denominators. Instead, he will encourage his students to use the pattern blocks to develop their own ways of solving the problems using fair trades and equivalent fractions. He feels this will provide a solid foundation for development of procedural under-standing in future grades.

Discussion

This vignette, like the first one, illustrates a lesson plan implemented by an experienced teacher, one who pays close attention to the many different factors that make up a successful learning experience. In this lesson, fourth graders have been learning about equivalent fractions in a hands-on manner using pattern blocks, a well-known and versatile manipulative. Most fourth graders have the basic skills to find equivalent fractions procedurally, yet Mr. Callahan decided that a conceptual understanding should come first. His method allowed them to investigate equivalent fractions at an appropriate level and created a foundation for more formal learning later.

Communication was a critical component. Plenty of small-group as well as whole-class discussion took place throughout the lesson. One of the great strengths of this activity lies in Mr. Callahan's ability to discuss the results of the activity with his students. Notice that his presentation did not seem rigid and overplanned in terms of the delivery. Rather, he used the comments of his students to guide him in his remarks, next steps, and pacing. For example, when students were confused about how to find another representation of $^2/_3$ using the pattern blocks, he did not simply tell them the answer and proceed with the next item on his lesson plan. He stopped to refocus the students on the concept of fair trade using the money example and allowed time for students to think about how his example related to the pattern blocks. Mr. Callahan has stepped back from the traditional role of teacher as lecturer and has taken on more of a facilitator role. He skillfully used classroom discourse to encourage active learning by not answering his own questions or even responding to students' comments with more information. Instead he encouraged them to reason through the questions themselves and construct their own understanding.

Note that there were a variety of instructional materials and methods used in order to include all of his learners, even those with special needs. English language learners' and special needs students' specific needs were addressed by using strategic groupings and multiple avenues to see the mathematics in different ways. He used various teaching techniques, such as active participation in solving problems, concrete and pictorial representations of the fractions, and verbal discussion of the results.

It is important to note that this lesson did not progress exactly as Mr. Callahan had planned. In reality, few lessons do. Mr. Callahan was able to use feedback from his class as a way to informally assess the direction and pacing of the lesson and adjust it accordingly. This type of on-the-spot adjustment is typical of those made by teachers every day, and it reflects the uniqueness of the makeup of students in each class.

SUCCESS IN TEACHING MATHEMATICS

In these two examples, both Miss Barilla and Mr. Callahan demonstrate a commitment to high-quality mathematics instruction for their students. Many of the strategies they implemented have been identified by experts as best practices in teaching mathematics. On the basis of current research and beliefs on the teaching and learning of mathematics (Grouws & Cebulla, 2000; National Association for Gifted Children, 2005; Tucson

Unified School District, n.d.), there is general consensus that the following statements are in line with best practices in teaching mathematics:

1. Meaningful mathematics should be taught in a problem-solving environment that balances both conceptual and procedural understanding of mathematics.

2. All students should be given the same opportunities to learn high-quality mathematics.

3. Communication, both verbal and written, should be a means to facilitate students' reflection and clarification of their own understanding.

4. Students should be engaged in constructing their own learning.

5. Mathematics should be presented in a developmentally appropriate manner, using a variety of instructional methods and suitable support, such as technology and manipulatives.

6. Assessment for both instruction and evaluation should be an integral part of instruction.

7. Attention to beliefs and attitudes related to learning mathematics should be addressed throughout instruction.

SUMMARY

This chapter has provided a glimpse of what some of the many facets of successful teaching and learning of mathematics look like. The two examples describe classrooms in which teachers are flexible, listen carefully to their students, and adjust the discourse to support student progress and success. The importance of these features will be discussed in detail throughout the book so as to further support a new teacher's ability to master them in the classroom.

2 Standards-Based Teaching

In Chapter 1, we presented two examples of teaching that provide insight into many successful methods used for teaching mathematics. The seven concluding statements on best practices were stated broadly, and several encompassed more than one idea. In this chapter we discuss standards to guide the content that you will teach in elementary school. These standards contain valuable information on what mathematics to teach, how to teach them, and what principles should guide your teaching. It is no coincidence that many of the best practices highlighted in Chapter 1 are included in the standards as well. Those broad ideas are described in much more specific terms in the standards documents. In this chapter we revisit these useful practices and situate them within the documents that present standards for teaching mathematics. We also provide examples of standards-based teaching in Grades K–6 in order, again, to offer some clear pictures of successful instruction that can be adapted for your own classroom success and that of your students.

WHY DO WE NEED STANDARDS FOR TEACHING MATHEMATICS?

Standards in any content area are designed to help establish what students should learn at each grade level or grade band. Standards typically stipulate the skills, concepts, and knowledge that are achievable. They should be used, in turn, to build criteria for assessments and establish goals for learning. Standards-based teaching is also an attempt to ensure that all students receive a high level of education in the area of mathematics. The National Council of Teachers of Mathematics (NCTM) has developed some guidelines to support this philosophy, and many states and districts have in turn created their own guidelines. As a new teacher, you will be given standards for the mathematics level you will teach and for other content you may be teaching.

THE NATIONAL COUNCIL OF TEACHERS OF MATHEMATICS PRINCIPLES AND STANDARDS

In 1989, NCTM first published its recommendations for the teaching and learning of K–12 mathematics. These recommendations were subsequently revisited and revised to inform the current document, the *Principles and Standards for School Mathematics* (NCTM, 2000). This document presents six principles (equity, curriculum, teaching, learning, assessment, and technology) and ten standards (number and operations, algebra, geometry, measurement, data analysis and probability, problem solving, reasoning and proof, communication, connections, and representations), which make up a framework for a high-quality mathematics education.

Principles

The six principles represent an overall philosophy for teaching and learning mathematics:

- *Equity.* This principle supports the view that there should be high expectations and strong support for all students.
- *Curriculum.* The curriculum principle refers to having a cohesive curriculum that focuses on important mathematics, clearly articulated across the grades. The curriculum principle is very important, as it demonstrates the need to have all students learn important mathematics in a consistent manner. Prior to this document, the mathematics taught varied widely as there was no general consensus on what and how to teach. Now, with these Principles and Standards, we have a clearer picture to guide teachers in the process of selecting the mathematics to be taught and methods to be used.
- *Teaching.* Effective teaching requires an understanding of what students know and what they need to know and then challenging and supporting them to learn it well.
- *Learning.* It is important for teachers to use knowledge of their students, and of teaching and learning mathematics, in order to

appropriately engage them in learning important mathematics. Learning should build on students' prior understanding, and students should be active in their own learning.

- *Assessment.* Assessment should support the learning of meaningful mathematics and be informative for both the student and the teacher. More detail on assessment can be found in Chapter 5.
- *Technology.* Essential to teaching and learning mathematics is the use of technology. Technology can influence content as well as pedagogy and can enhance the learning process (NCTM, 2000).

Content and Process Standards

The ten standards are broken down into two groups, which speak to what to teach as well as how to teach it. Five mathematical content strands describe the content students should learn: number and operations, algebra, geometry, measurement, and data analysis and probability. Five mathematical processes highlight the ways of acquiring and using the content knowledge: problem solving, reasoning and proof, communication, connections, and representation.

The Five Content Standards

1. Number and Operations

This content standard encompasses the understanding of numbers and number systems. According to this standard, students should be knowledgeable about ways of representing numbers and the relationships among numbers, and they should understand the meaning of operations and how they relate to one another. Students should also be able to compute fluently and make reasonable estimates.

2. Algebra

Algebra is an important topic that can be integrated across the grades, beginning in elementary school. Students should investigate patterns, relations, and functions. They should be able to represent and analyze mathematical situations and structures using algebraic symbols. They should use mathematical models to represent and understand quantitative relationships, as well as analyze change in various contexts. At the end of this chapter, we give examples for integrating algebraic thinking across the grades.

3. Geometry

NCTM standards reflect research that says geometry needs to be introduced at a young age. Students should analyze characteristics and properties of two- and three-dimensional geometric shapes and develop mathematical arguments about geometric relationships. They should be able to use coordinate geometry and other representational systems to describe spatial relationships. They should apply transformations and use symmetry to analyze mathematical situations and use visualization, spatial reasoning, and geometric modeling to solve problems.

4. Measurement

Like geometry, early exposure and integration of measurement concepts are essential. Students should understand measurable attributes of objects and the units, systems, and processes of measurement. They should apply appropriate techniques, tools, and formulas to determine measurements.

5. Data Analysis and Probability

Students should formulate questions that can be addressed with data and collect, organize, and display relevant data to answer them. They should be able to select and use appropriate statistical methods to analyze data as well as develop and evaluate inferences and predictions that are based on data. They should also understand and apply basic concepts of probability.

The Five Process Standards

1. Problem Solving

Because problem solving can be challenging for students, it is important to provide multiple opportunities and to do so in a meaningful context. Students need frequent experience with solving problems in a variety of contexts. According to NCTM (2000), students should be able to build new mathematical knowledge through problem solving. As students solve meaningful problems, they should solidify the mathematics they already know, extend their knowledge to include more mathematics, and develop fluency with skills. To help students bridge from existing to new knowledge, skillful teachers encourage students to apply and adapt a variety of appropriate strategies to solve a problem. In addition, students need to be provided with explicit strategies, such as Polya's Four Step Process for Problem Solving (Polya, 1945) or STAR, also for problem solving. Polya's four-step process is as follows:

1. Understand the problem.

2. Devise a plan.

3. Carry out the plan.

4. Look back.

STAR is another first-letter mnemonic that is effective for general problem solving (Maccini & Hughes, 2000):

Search the word problem (read the problem carefully; write down the facts).

Translate the words into an equation in picture form (e.g., choose a variable, identify the operation, and represent the problem through manipulatives or picture form).

Answer the problem.

Review the solution (e.g., reread the problem; check for reasonableness of the answer).

In addition, students should also be given the opportunity to monitor and reflect on the process of mathematical problem solving.

Recall the use of real-world problems used in the second grade vignette. Students were asked to use the base-ten blocks to model and solve the given problems. Students also demonstrated a variety of approaches in their problem solving by making the connections between addition and subtraction.

2. Reasoning and Proof

Although it is important that students know how to *do* mathematics, it is also critical that they understand *why* they are doing what they are doing. This process standard suggests that reasoning and proof are fundamental aspects of mathematics and that students should regularly investigate mathematical conjectures, evaluate mathematical arguments, and use a variety of methods of reasoning and proof. One of the features of the fourth grade example was the use of reasoning to determine why two out of three blue rhombuses ($^2/_3$) is equivalent to four out of six green triangles ($^4/_6$).

3. Communication

Understanding tends to be more complete when students are required to explain, elaborate, or defend their position to others. Throughout both examples in Chapter 1, students were fully involved in communicating their mathematical understanding. Communications were given room for expression in small-group discussion, whole-class discussions and presentations, and written form. Developing habits of verbalizing and writing mathematical examples and procedures can greatly help in removing obstacles to success in general mathematics settings. Advocates of writing in the disciplines believe it is a tool that helps students think better (Pugalee, 1997; Sierpinska, 1998) as they produce, apply, and extend knowledge to make sense for themselves in the same way that mathematicians and scientists do (Connolly, 1989). It is not always easy for students to communicate their personal understandings, but one of the most rewarding efforts a teacher can make is to begin early to help them to develop this skill.

4. Connections

Hiebert and Carpenter (1992) state that the degree of a student's understanding is determined by the number, accuracy, and strength of connections he or she makes. Connections should be made and used within and among areas of mathematics as well as to other subject areas. For example, connections were made in the vignettes between the inverse operations of addition and subtraction as well as between conceptual and procedural understanding of equivalent fractions. As teachers grow in their experience, these connections will become more visible to them and can be reinforced for their students.

5. Representation

"The ways in which mathematical ideas are represented is [sic] fundamental to how people can understand and use those ideas" (NCTM, 2000, p. 67). Using multiple representations involves communicating mathematics in different ways. For example, when teaching the concept of subtraction with regrouping, Miss Barilla used the base-ten blocks as a concrete representation of the problem situation. Mr. Callahan incorporated pattern blocks as a concrete representation of fractions and their equivalence. Students used pictures as well as symbols to represent their fractions. Students learning mathematics often need multiple methods of viewing a concept in order to understand it. As students develop their understanding of mathematics, their repertoire of representations increases and becomes more varied. Students with special needs and English language learners can particularly benefit from use of multiple representations (Chapter 3 expands on this thought).

These principles, content standards, and process standards offer a clear framework with which to guide your instruction. Greater detail is provided in the document itself. To read a full description, go to www.nctm.org or obtain *Principles and Standards for School Mathematics* written by NCTM (2000). The standards are divided into grade bands (PreK–2, 3–5, 6–8, and 9–12) and provide specific examples of how these standards look at each of the grade levels.

STATE AND DISTRICT STANDARDS FOR TEACHING MATHEMATICS

As mentioned earlier, most states have created their own sets of state standards, often written with the NCTM Standards as guidelines. In addition, each school district frequently writes its own standards, and these in turn are usually based on the respective state standards. Typically, the NCTM Standards are more general than either state or district standards and written in multiple grade-level bands, whereas many state and district standards give specifics as to what skills and concepts should be taught at each grade level. As a new teacher of mathematics, it can be very confusing to sift through all of these documents. Yet it is important to familiarize yourself with them before your first day of class. Copies should be readily available to you from your principal, your mathematics department chair, or the mathematics curriculum specialist for the district.

THE RELATIONSHIP BETWEEN STANDARDS AND STANDARDS-BASED MATHEMATICS TEXTBOOKS

Many of the popular mathematics textbooks are now written to address current mathematics standards. These are often listed in the textbook or the supplemental material that accompanies the text. Although you may take great comfort in the thought that all the hard work of matching standards to curricula has been done for you, please be sure to read through the standards documents yourself, to be sure they are included in your text as intended by your school or district standards. Even though the textbook you are using may be standards based, it may not contain all of your grade-level standards, or it may contain higher or lower grade-level standards. You want to make sure your standards correlate with the textbook.

NCTM CURRICULUM FOCAL POINTS

If you find the idea of dozens of individual standards for mathematics at each grade level overwhelming, do not despair. Each standard does not have to be addressed in isolation, and many of them are written toward a common goal. In fact, there are a few key concepts that are critical at each grade level. These have been identified in *Curriculum Focal Points* (NCTM, 2006). This document addresses the most important mathematics taught at each level and seeks unity among the different individual state documents regarding mathematics standards. For each grade level, three curriculum focal points are given that consist of related knowledge, skills, and concepts.

For example, let's take a look at the three focal points for third grade:

Number and Operations and Algebra: Developing understandings of multiplication and division and strategies for basic multiplication facts and related division facts

Number and Operations: Developing an understanding of fractions and fraction equivalence

Geometry: Describing and analyzing properties of two-dimensional shapes

These are the big ideas in third grade. And the focal points for fourth grade build upon them:

Number and Operations and Algebra: Developing quick recall of multiplication facts and related division facts and fluency with whole number multiplication

Number and Operations: Developing an understanding of decimals, including the connections between fractions and decimals

Measurement: Developing an understanding of area and determining the areas of two-dimensional shapes

These focal points can help you to organize and prioritize the list of standards by providing a core set of topics at each grade level. Although the focal points are not meant to be followed at the expense of excluding other standards, they do help you to keep the most important topics front and center. These are the topics that need to be understood thoroughly for success in future mathematics.

EXAMPLES OF STANDARDS-BASED ACTIVITIES INVOLVING ALGEBRAIC THINKING

When planning standards-based instruction, it is important to familiarize yourself with the standards for the grades before and after the one you are teaching in order to better understand the development of concepts across grades. Such broader understanding enables you to build upon prior knowledge at an appropriate level for your students and to provide a proper foundation for future learning. This knowledge will also accumulate over time as you gain experience as a teacher and communicate with teachers of other grade levels.

One important content area that begins in elementary school and is developed across the grade levels is algebra. When we think of algebra, we traditionally think of solving an equation for *x*. In Grades K–6, however, most students are not developmentally ready for such abstract thought and computation. However, they *can* begin thinking algebraically at a developmentally appropriate level. To promote such thinking, elementary students should encounter algebra in a much less formal manner, one that involves concrete and pictorial models.

Jerome Bruner (1966), one of the best-known and most influential educational psychologists of the twentieth century, noted that learners develop understanding of a concept by moving through three distinct modes of learning: (1) enactive, (2) iconic, and (3) symbolic. These terms could be translated as (1) using concrete manipulatives, (2) using pictures, and (3) using numbers or symbols.

When teaching a younger student, for example, you are most likely to teach concepts in a concrete, hands-on manner. Bruner advocated using manipulatives with younger students so that they can physically perform the actions represented by the mathematical symbols. Students would then progress to the pictorial stage, in which they would draw pictures of the actions instead of actually performing them. The final stage, the symbolic stage, involves the use of numbers and mathematical symbols to represent the quantities and actions implied by the pictures. These stages correspond to the process standard of representation advocated by NCTM. We offer some examples from Grades K–6 on how ideas from algebra can be introduced, revisited, and used as a foundation to build upon across the elementary grades. These examples are ideas for developing lessons based on standards set by NCTM, in light of Bruner's philosophy.

Overview of Lessons

Across these activities you will see the incorporation of Bruner's philosophy that learners develop understanding of a concept by moving through three distinct modes of learning: concrete manipulatives, pictorial, and symbolic. To incorporate Bruner's enactive stage of learning into each activity, students are asked to build a concrete representation of the problem situation using manipulatives, which enables them to physically explore the mathematics. Although

Three distinct modes of learning

1. Concrete—hands-on
2. Pictorial
3. Symbolic—numbers or symbols

this step is more critical with young students, the benefits of this stage should not be overlooked with older students. Very young students may not progress beyond the concrete stage, yet each of these activities allows for progression to the pictorial stage by drawing pictures to represent the concrete models as well as using symbols to represent the problem situation (symbolic stage).

Kindergarten: Day and Night

One facet of algebraic thinking is the study of patterns. Students in kindergarten are exposed to repeating patterns, such as red, blue, red, blue, and so forth. In this activity, students are required to place the block of either a sun or moon to continue the pattern. (Note: If you do not have actual sun and moon objects in your classroom, you may adapt this pattern to include concrete objects that you possess. One option is to use two different colors of candy in your pattern.)

Kindergarten students can work with blocks or real objects to create a repeating pattern using two shapes. Students should be able to complete the repeating pattern and then progress to patterns that include more than two shapes. Students can also develop their own patterns using blocks or pictures and trade their patterns with a classmate to continue the pattern.

First and Second Grades: Bigger and Bigger Blocks

In the first and second grades, students continue their experiences with repeating patterns and can begin to investigate growing patterns. If your students are struggling with growing patterns, have them revisit an easier problem using patterns such as the Day and Night problem. The following pattern is accessible to these grade levels.

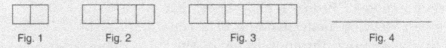

| Fig. 1 | Fig. 2 | Fig. 3 | Fig. 4 |

Students are given pictures of the first three figures in the pattern and are asked to determine the next figure. Possible questions for discussion are as follows:

1. How many blocks does Figure 5 have? Figure 8? Figure 10? Students can determine the answer to these questions in several ways, depending on their developmental level. For many first graders, it is sufficient to build the figures one at a time, adding two blocks to the previous figure. Stronger first graders and many second graders may be able to solve this problem by counting by twos.

2. Can there be seven squares in a figure? Explain why or why not. This question can be investigated by trial and error as students use the blocks to help them decide if such a figure is possible. Questions like this lay the foundation for solving abstract equations,

such as $2x = 7$. For many first graders, it is sufficient to build the blocks as before or count by twos in order to determine that you can never get to seven this way. Stronger first graders and many second graders may be able to investigate a more difficult question, such as whether a figure with twenty-one blocks is possible.

3. What patterns do you notice? There are many patterns, and the purpose of this question is to encourage students to look for relationships among the sequence of blocks as well as the sequence of numbers produced. Encourage exploration of all patterns, whether or not they lend themselves to the solution of one of the questions you have posed. Some patterns are as follows:

   a. Two blocks are added each time to create the next figure.
   b. All the figures will have an *even* number of blocks. (This activity provides an ideal time to introduce or reinforce the number theory concepts of *even* and *odd*.)
   c. The number of blocks is twice as large as (or double) the figure number. Most students at this level will not see this pattern, and it should be considered a challenge. You could challenge your students to find a way to determine how many blocks are in a figure if you only know the figure number. This line of questioning lays the groundwork for determining the formula that represents the given pattern ($y = 2x$ in this case), which will not be addressed using symbols until a later grade.

Another pattern that goes along with these ideas is that of odd numbers.

| Fig. 1 | Fig. 2 | Fig. 3 | Fig. 4 |

Similar questions can be asked. Two blocks are still being added each time, yet the pattern produced is of odd numbers. It will be harder for the students to determine a relationship between the figure number and the number of blocks ($y = 2x + 1$).

Third Through Sixth Grades: Time for a Party

A classic algebraic problem is that of seating people at a party using square tables that can fit exactly one person on each side. The following problem is one that can be adapted and extended for many grade levels.

A child is having a party and needs to know how many tables to set up to accommodate the guests. The pictures show that one table can accommodate four people and two tables placed together can accommodate six people.

Students in third through sixth grades can be asked to use manipulatives to determine how many people can be seated using three, four, and five tables. If necessary, students can continue to use manipulatives to create the tables for larger numbers of people. Building on the activities from the first and second grades, students in third through sixth grades can further their understanding of growing patterns by (1) answering more difficult questions about table sizes they have not built, (2) organizing their findings in a table (T-chart), and (3) exploring the generalization of the pattern in words, symbols, or a combination of words and symbols. This activity still makes use of the "+2" pattern from the first and second grade activity, but the generalization ($y = 2x + 2$) is slightly more complex. It expands the patterns represented by the previous even ($y = 2x$) and odd ($y = 2x + 1$) patterns.

Possible questions for discussion are as follows. Remember that you can change the numbers to be smaller or larger depending on the ability level of your class.

1. Organize your findings in a table (T-chart) to represent the number of people who can be seated when the number of tables ranges from 1 to 5 (or 1 to 10). Some students may choose to draw the pictures instead of building them with the blocks. This step allows them to have a record that can be referred to after the blocks have been put away.

2. If there are 12 (or 20) tables, how many people can you seat? This question involves some abstract thought, because students will not actually build the pattern this far. Students need to develop a method involving multiplication and addition: that of multiplying the number of tables by 2 to represent people sitting on either side of the table and then adding 2 to represent the people on the ends.

3. If there are 22 (or 30) people, how many tables would you need? To solve this problem, students need to undo the method they used in Question 2—first subtract 2, and then divide by 2.

4. Can you seat 15 (or 25) people with no empty seats? Explain.

5. What patterns do you notice? Explain each pattern. Students should observe that the number of people increases by two each time a table is added. (Discussion should

include why the number of people doesn't increase by four, even though there are four sides to each table.) Students may observe that the number of people that can be seated is always an even number. They may also observe that, regardless of the number of tables, there are always two people seated on the ends. If you take away these two people, then the number of people seated is twice the number of tables. (Remember that this idea of multiplying by two is the first pattern in the first and second grade example.)

6. What generalizations can you make about the relationship between the number of tables and the number of people seated? Students can explain the relationship in words; a few students may be ready to write the formula.

For students who are ready to extend their learning, here are some possible extensions.

1. This problem can be extended by using rectangular instead of square tables. The shape of the table can also be changed to a triangle, hexagon, or octagon. Students can build these patterns and investigate how the shape of the table affects the number of people that can be seated.

2. This activity can be used to investigate perimeter and area. Students can be asked to determine relationships between the perimeter and the number of tables used, as well as the relationship between area and the number of tables.

NCTM Standards Addressed

Looking back at the NCTM content and process standards and the manner in which these standards were incorporated into the algebra activities, it is worth noting that although the discussed activities included more than one process standard, not every lesson you teach will include all of the process standards. However, it is important to strive to incorporate as many process standards as possible over the course of a unit.

Content Standards

The activities described primarily address the algebra content standard, specifically the focus on understanding patterns, relations, and functions. Students use mathematical models to represent and understand a quantitative relationship. The upper elementary students represent and analyze mathematical situations and structures using algebraic symbols.

The secondary content strand is that of number and operations. In the first and second grade activity, counting by twos is used as a strategy, and the concept of even and odd numbers is included. In the third through sixth grade activity, students incorporate arithmetic operations to determine the answer to questions such as, "If there are twenty tables, how many people can you seat?"

Process Standards

Problem solving: These activities are nonroutine problems, and as such, they require students to use their knowledge in different ways. Problem solving is used throughout the activities as the students apply a variety of appropriate strategies, such as drawing pictures and finding patterns, to solve the problem situations.

Reasoning and Proof: Students use reasoning to develop methods to continue the pattern without actually building it. They must also construct arguments showing that certain cases are not possible. For example, in the first through second grade activity, students can prove that there is no figure with 7 squares by creating the figures with 6 and 8 tiles and explaining the pattern of adding two.

Communication: In each of these lessons, students can work in groups. Mathematical understanding can be communicated both orally, during small-group and whole-group interactions, as well as in written form, when responding to questions on a handout created by the teacher.

Connections: Connections can be made among the visual and numerical representations of the problem situation. The mathematical concepts of algebra and number and operations are also connected in these activities.

Representation: Students use concrete models and pictures to represent the problem situations at all ages. Upper elementary students use tables (T-charts) and other means to organize information and translate between representations to answer questions related to the problem situation.

Many of the same ideas from the list of best practices in Chapter 1 are reflected in the NCTM Standards just cited. It is important to mention again that these best practices, as well as the NCTM Standards, are intended to guide you as you develop your curricula for *all* of your learners. The process of setting high standards for all students should include planning instruction based on the same age-appropriate curriculum and activities and does not mean that you teach a different set of objectives to part of your class. You should use the same goals and base curriculum for all of your students. Students who are lagging behind in basic skills or concepts should not use a different curriculum; they should just have opportunities to learn the curriculum in different ways.

In the coming chapters we discuss strategies that may be used to differentiate your instruction to include all learners yet still provide the same high-quality, standards-based instruction for your learners.

SUMMARY

In this chapter, we discussed essential information about standards-based teaching in mathematics and some examples of standards-based activities. We want to emphasize the importance of incorporating both the process standards as well as the content standards in your curricula. Traditionally, schools have focused on teaching the content via procedures and basic skills; however, equally important are the process standards that focus on critical thinking and problem solving, reasoning, communication, representations, and making connections to support learning. The parallels between the algebra lessons provided here and the two vignettes from Chapter 1 demonstrate the link between current research on best practices for teaching and the standards for teaching a subject, which *should* go hand in hand.

As you grow in your teaching, one of the best steps you can take is to increase your awareness of and attention to the process strands so that you may consciously incorporate them increasingly in your future teaching. These important standards are frequently overlooked in the teaching of mathematics.

3
Engaging Students in Learning Mathematics

*Students are engaged when they are interested—challenged—
satisfied—persistent—and committed to their school work.*

—Center for Leadership in School Reform

Over the next several years as a teacher, you will begin to develop your philosophy on classroom management. You have no doubt read about some of the many strategies of classroom management and have probably also begun to consider how these strategies fit in with your style of teaching. We would like to suggest in this chapter that the real issue is not management, but engagement—engagement within the topics that you teach and in the manner in which you teach them. If lessons are interesting, challenging, meaningful, and include all learners, students will be engaged in the learning process, and classroom disruptions can be minimized.

In Chapter 1, when Miss Barilla praised her students for their efforts and posted mathematics papers on the wall, she was encouraging her students to have a positive attitude about learning mathematics. In the vignette, the students are all actively participating in their activities. New teachers will find, however, that such engagement must be nurtured and developed over time. Furthermore, there are issues specific to teaching and learning mathematics that can directly impact your students' abilities to engage in the tasks you set before them. These issues are reflective both of students' real mathematical abilities as well as their perceptions of those abilities and whether or not they themselves are an integral part of your classroom.

WHAT IS ENGAGEMENT?

According to Pintrich and Schrauben (1992), student engagement consists of three interrelated components: affective, behavioral, and cognitive. Affective factors include student interest in learning as well as the beliefs and emotions tied to their experiences in learning a particular subject. Behavioral factors include actions that can be observed, such as participation in a particular activity and communicating with group members while solving a problem. Cognitive factors involve the mental effort and processing expended while learning something new. So students who are sufficiently engaged in a mathematics lesson display positive emotions toward learning mathematics, actively participate in the activities of the day, and exhibit a dedication to think deeply about a given problem.

As we begin to discuss strategies within the three components of engagement, you may notice overlaps. These components are interrelated, and strategies for one often support the development of one or both of the others. For example, a teacher who uses strategies to develop a positive classroom culture (affective component) will also generally impact the students' participation (behavioral component), and thus the students' ability to think about and learn a new concept (cognitive component). Promoting engagement in your classroom is no small feat, however. In this chapter we talk about these three interrelated components and provide insight on how you can encourage your students to be fully engaged in their learning.

ENGAGING LEARNERS IN THE AFFECTIVE DOMAIN

Let's consider Around the World and Math Jeopardy, two classic games played when teaching mathematics.

Vignette 1: Third Grade Multiplication—Around the World

Miss Riviera uses the game Around the World to increase her student's fluency with multiplication facts. In this popular elementary game, the teacher holds up an arithmetic fact on a flash card while students compete in pairs to be the first to respond with the answer. The winner gets to move to the desk of the next student and challenge him or her, while the loser sits down. A good player can effectively "go around the world" (the classroom), moving on to challenge one student after the next. Gina, a strong student with a great deal of mathematical confidence, monopolizes the entire game with her quick responses to arithmetic facts. Most of her peers sit and watch passively as she demonstrates her knowledge. There is little incentive to try to beat Gina when students have lost to her numerous times before. Miss Riviera had intended this to be a fun game, recalling her fondness for the game as a third grader herself. Yet she can't ignore her observations that this game is not accomplishing her goal of having everyone practice their multiplication facts.

Vignette 2: Fifth Grade—Math Jeopardy

Mr. Hammond, a fifth grade teacher, likes to review for mathematics tests with games. The game he has chosen today is based on the popular television show Jeopardy, *in which a clue is given and contestants have to come up with the answer. Higher point values are attached to the more difficult clues. In mathematics classes, students generally play the game in teams, and the first team to get the correct answer wins the advertised number of points. Mr. Hammond divides his class into teams and proceeds with the game. After a few rounds it is apparent that Heriberto's group has taken a commanding lead, and the rest of the class begins to make comments to that effect. "Heriberto solves all the problems quicker than we can, Mr. Hammond. It's not fair!" Mr. Hammond continues without comment and finishes the game, but he wonders how effective it was in reviewing the important material from the chapter.*

These two examples are typical of scenarios played out by well-meaning teachers who are seeking to vary their instructional practices in mathematics. Their intentions are noble, yet it is often the case that, even when teachers are aware that the activity is not quite what they intended, they are at a loss when it comes to making improvements. The primary issue here is that of engagement: how to ensure that each student is participating in the learning process as fully as possible. This leads us to consider the general philosophy of Glasser's (1992) Five Basic Needs.

A Description of Glasser's Five Basic Needs

A positive classroom environment is an essential component of teaching. The classroom climate that you create in the beginning of the school year will help to influence how comfortable your students will feel partic-ipating in your instructional activities. If the climate you have created is warm and welcoming, students will be more likely to try new experiences without fear of failure or ridicule. This is especially important in mathe-matics, in which many students have experienced failure and mathemat-ics anxiety.

Glasser (1992) believes that all human beings have the same basic needs. He categorizes them into five categories: (1) survival, (2) love and belonging, (3) fun, (4) freedom, and (5) power. He also describes how each of these basic needs is reflected in the classroom.

The first need is the most basic: survival. This need encompasses everything necessary to live, such as food, water, shelter, and clothing. This basic need must be met before any learning can take place. Students who are struggling to survive will not be able to focus on school, much less on learning mathematics. If your students are coming to school hungry or sleepy, for example, it may be a sign that some of these basic needs are not being met. For the next four basic needs, a teacher can seek to meet them in his or her mathematics classroom in simple, yet effective ways.

The need for love and belonging may be the most obvious. Students who feel that their teachers like them are more likely to put forth effort in the classroom. Furthermore, students who feel that their teacher not only likes them but is also interested in their lives will feel more connected to their classroom. Allowing for a few minutes of sharing during the week helps everyone to get to know each other better, thus creating a sense of community between teacher and students. In addition, decorating the walls with work done by your students tells them that their work is important enough to be displayed and that they have played a part in the way their room looks. (Notice that we said "their" room, and not "your" room. If you really want your students to feel like they belong, you should refer to it this way as well.) For example, there are many opportunities to incorporate mathematics with other subject areas, such as art. Mathematics projects, homework, and other work are excellent examples of finished products that may be displayed on bulletin boards and walls around the classroom.

The third basic need—fun—is easy enough to supply. There are numer-ous opportunities for fun when learning mathematics. They can be as simple as telling a funny story as a lead-in to your lesson, using a favorite manipulative to learn a new mathematics concept, or incorporating a math-ematics game as a review. Learning may be serious business, but don't miss the chance to sprinkle it with a bit of fun as frequently as possible.

The fourth need, freedom, takes some explaining in this context. Freedom in a classroom may be exhibited by students choosing the edu-cational activities they will work on after finishing an assignment, such as exploring educational software related to mathematics or doing a mathematics puzzle. They can be given the freedom to choose their own seats or to choose their own partners for a particular project. Even a regular, optional challenge assignment gives students freedom to do only the optional assignments that are really interesting to them.

The last basic need, power, can better be described as competence or success in the classroom. Students who feel that they are good at mathematics will feel empowered in your classroom, be less likely to fear asking "stupid" questions, and be more willing to present solutions on the board. This feeling of competence comes from students' perceived view of how others see them—both the teacher and classmates. Students gain power or rank in the classroom in various ways. An experienced teacher such as Mrs. Smith may make a point to give out certificates to each person who receives an "A" on a test. Another teacher, Mr. Cayman, likes to name good ideas after the person who suggested them, and he also posts these good ideas up on the wall. When he is solving a problem during class, he will often be heard saying, "Oh, here's where we need to use Suzy's solution." Every time Suzy's solution is mentioned, her mathematical power increases.

A word of caution: It is important to understand that increasing students' feelings of power in your classroom should be one of your highest-level goals, and students who are empowered in mathematics can accomplish truly amazing things, far beyond what you can probably imagine at this point. Yet in your quest to instill power in your classroom, don't make the inexperienced teacher's mistake of widening the gap between the haves and the have-nots. Your brightest students, the ones who always get the "A's" and thus always receive the certificates, are not the ones you necessarily need to empower.

There are ways to empower the rest of the learners as well. Let's consider the case of Miss Gold and her student Rich, who is struggling in her mathematics class.

Vignette 3: Increasing a Student's Confidence in Mathematics

Seeing that Rich was having some trouble understanding, Miss Gold asked him to come in for extra help. When she helped him solve a problem, she let him know that she would ask him to write his solution on the board the next day. The next day, she assigned several problems to be written and explained on the board, making sure she included the problem she had discussed with Rich the day before. Rich solved his assigned problem beautifully and seemed very happy and confident of his work. Over the next few weeks, he continued to ask Miss Gold for help and volunteered to put more problems on the board.

The strategy used by Miss Gold allowed Rich to demonstrate his correct solution to the class without having to reveal to his peers that he had received help on this problem the day before. As a result of this one step toward improving confidence, Miss Gold helped Rich to feel better about his mathematical abilities. Rich then began to take responsibility for his own learning by continuing to ask for help. By volunteering to put more problems on the board, he increased his power in the class, thus developing stronger feelings of competence. By one simple action, Miss Gold had encouraged Rich to take more initiative in his learning and to believe in himself and in his success in mathematics. That is the kind of power a teacher should ultimately be seeking to promote.

A Fresh Look at Around the World and Math Jeopardy

Now that we have described Glasser's (1992) Five Basic Needs, let's revisit the two popular mathematics activities: Around the World and Math Jeopardy. Recall that Miss Riviera was unsatisfied with the outcome of the Around the World game she used to practice multiplication facts in her third grade class. Gina seemed to be the only one who really obtained much practice at all, and she didn't really need the practice as much as some of the other students in her class.

Miss Riviera had just finished reading about Glasser's Five Basic Needs (a book suggested by her principal) and she began to reflect on these needs in light of the game her students had just played. What she began to realize was that, apart from Gina, most of the students' needs for fun were not being addressed. In addition, Gina was the only student who was able to feel confident (powerful) about her mathematical knowledge. This game, unbeknownst to Miss Riviera, actually served to decrease the power of everyone else in the class. What Miss Riviera learned from this experience is that, before implementing an activity in her classroom, she needs to take into consideration the needs of all of her students, not just a few. This is not to say that Around the World is an ineffective activity. Rather, it should be balanced with other activities that engage more of the class. She decided to use this game once in a while but to also try things like putting students in groups of two to give each student more individual practice with flash cards.

It is also important to remember what was discussed earlier: The high-achieving student does not need help in becoming empowered as much as the average- or low-achieving student. It is often the case that we give out accolades to the *first* person to get the answer. What message does that send to many other students who may have been able to solve the problem, given a little more time? It may teach them not to try harder, because they believe they have very little chance of defeating the Ginas, who seem to *always* be the first ones to get it right.

Now let's look at the changes Mr. Hammond decided to make with his Math Jeopardy game. After reflecting on the outcomes, he came to the conclusion that this game did not encourage the majority of the class to work hard to solve the problems. Because it is a game of speed, the students who solve problems more slowly were not confident enough in their abilities to follow through in the problem, believing that the quicker students would beat them to the answer anyway. More often than not, one of the quicker students on each team was responsible for solving most of the problems correctly, while the others did little but become frustrated. Mr. Hammond took some time to consider the intended outcomes of this game. He hoped that this game would help students review the mathematics concepts in the unit and to increase students' confidence in the knowledge they had gained. As a secondary goal, he hoped his students would have fun solving the mathematics problems in a competitive atmosphere.

Finally, he made two seemingly minor rule changes. First, in order for a team to win points, *two* people on the team had to solve the problem. The second rule change was that once the winning team was awarded the points, all the other teams in the class could finish the problem for half the total points.

What was accomplished by these simple rules? They instituted very important principles for including everyone in the activity. First, because two team members must solve the problem, it sends out a clear message that everyone cannot simply rely on the smartest team member, that it truly is a group effort. Second, it partially takes the element of speed out of the equation, thus encouraging the rest of the class not to give up. Even though a group may not be the quickest in solving the problem, if they are diligent to finish, they have the chance to collect half the points. Thus, for each question, every team can feel successful by winning at least half the allotted points. By incorporating these simple rules, Mr. Hammond has taken a classic game dependent on speed and turned it into a game with more winners, thus promoting more positive feelings toward the mathematics game and, ultimately, more confidence in the students' mathematical abilities.

These two examples demonstrate how knowledge of Glasser's Five Basic Needs can be used to guide decisions on engaging all learners. Creating a classroom climate conducive to including every student can be accomplished by first considering what your goals are for each classroom activity. If your activity is not producing the intended outcomes, then you need to ask yourself this question: Which of the five basic needs is this activity not meeting for my students? As demonstrated earlier, the activity may only need some minor adjustments to increase student participation.

Glasser's Five Basic Needs
1. Survival
2. Love and belonging
3. Fun
4. Freedom
5. Power

Glasser's Five Basic Needs provides a foundation for our philosophy of engagement. If you consider the needs of the students in your class, and you design your lesson with their needs in mind, your intended outcome—that of including everyone in learning mathematics—will be closer to being realized. With Glasser's Five Basic Needs in mind, let's further inspect affective issues specific to the domain of mathematics.

AFFECTIVE ISSUES RELATED TO TEACHING AND LEARNING MATHEMATICS

You have seen that the Five Basic Needs are general in that they can relate to any classroom. Yet these needs have particular relevance in a mathematics classroom, where emotions play a big role in students' attitudes toward learning mathematics. Research has found that students' past experiences in learning mathematics influence their disposition toward further learning in this area (Sliva & Roddick, 2001). Before students arrive in a classroom, their mathematical experiences have helped to form their beliefs about their mathematical abilities. Students experience both positive and negative emotions while learning mathematics, and these emotions influence the development of their attitudes toward mathematics as a whole. Many students who are struggling with mathematics experience mathematics anxiety, which can prevent them from learning effectively in this field. It can be very challenging for both the student and the teacher to undo these feelings of anxiety toward the subject. Because affective variables can impact a student's learning of mathematics, strategies for fostering a positive attitude toward mathematics should be used in instruction.

Attitudes Toward Learning Mathematics

Four affective issues often arise when learning mathematics: (1) the role of the teacher; (2) support and influence of family; (3) challenge; and (4) issues of fear, failure, and avoidance (Sliva & Roddick, 2001). All four of these issues have great potential to influence a student's attitude toward learning mathematics and should be recognized as such. Throughout this book we focus on the role of the teacher in learning mathematics. In the section to follow, "Getting to Know Your Students," we briefly discuss the role of the family. We touched on the issues of challenge and fear when we discussed Glasser's Five Basic Needs, and we expand on these ideas here in relation to learning mathematics.

The issues of challenge and fear are ones that hit home for many students in mathematics classes. Challenge can be any situation in which students are asked to compete with themselves or their peers to demonstrate their understanding of mathematics topics. Many of these challenges are timed, which provokes even more anxiety in a student who is just learning new mathematical facts and concepts. One typical challenge is the previously discussed Around the World activity, in which students compete with each other on basic facts. Fear often results from failing at a given challenge, thus creating a desire to avoid such challenge and negative feelings in the future.

Of course, the use of challenge can be both positive and negative. For some students, the experience of having to compete with their peers is devastating and can create detrimental effects on their feelings toward mathematics and their perceived ability to learn the subject. These students may be fearful of any challenge and become afraid of failing in mathematics. For others, challenge is a driving force in shaping their positive attitudes toward mathematics. It is important for the teacher to be sensitive to each student's personality and how he or she responds to challenge, especially in mathematics.

Students whose last memory of learning mathematics resulted in fear or failure will likely have quite different perceptions about learning further mathematics than students who recall a more positive resolution to a difficult situation in a mathematics class. Above all, in addition to greater mathematical understandings, you, as a teacher, want your students to leave with fond memories of your mathematics class.

Because affective variables can impact a student's learning of mathematics, strategies for fostering a positive attitude toward the subject should be used in instruction. The following list is a compilation of instructional techniques for addressing affective issues (Mercer & Mercer, 1998; Montague, 1997):

- Involve students in setting their own goals and support students in understanding their responsibility and role in their own learning. If students are engaged in determining their own learning goals, they often begin to take personal responsibility for their learning rather then seeing it as something out of their control. These goals should be challenging yet attainable.

- Make learning meaningful. Provide problems that are relevant to students' lives, so that they connect with the mathematics you are teaching.
- Model enthusiasm toward learning and doing mathematics.
- Have students write about their attitudes and feelings toward mathematics.
- Provide the opportunity for students to demonstrate what they have learned for other students, and teach them to compliment one another for trying hard and being successful.
- Deemphasize goals that foster competition among students. Avoid publicizing grades based on comparisons among students.

Because students differ in their motivation, self-perception, and attitudes, strategies for increasing positive attitudes toward learning mathematics will vary, depending on the student. An important component in maintaining a positive attitude toward learning mathematics is to create a classroom environment that is conducive to learning for all students. Students must feel that if they fail, they will not be punished or ridiculed by the teacher or other peers. A discussion in the first few days of school about the types of behavior that are acceptable in the class should also include specifics about how students are to treat each other. Mistakes should be treated as avenues to success.

Getting to Know Your Students

It is important to recognize the influence of the family on students' beliefs about learning mathematics. Contacting parents or guardians of the student may be very useful in determining more about the lives of the student outside of school. Often, learning about home expectations can provide a new perspective on how to more effectively teach the student. Some basic affective information you may gather from parents or guardians may be geared toward whether the student appears to have a positive disposition toward learning mathematics. For information about going a step further and seeking the support and involvement of parents in students learning mathematics, see Appendix A.

As well as information gathered before you meet your students, there is also valuable information to be gathered after you meet the students. You may want to spend time one on one with them, inquiring about their past experiences learning mathematics and what they would like to achieve for themselves as mathematical learners. You may want them to respond in journals about similar experiences (depending on their ages), or observe them learning mathematics individually in small and large groups. Asking students about their preferences when learning mathematics can provide a unique insight that other sources of information about the students are lacking.

As a teacher, it is important to be understanding and flexible about the needs your students may have. These efforts will go a long way toward gaining their respect and the support of parents and guardians. Many students may not come from homes with parents who can help them with mathematics homework or projects; some may come from homes where English is not the first language or is spoken at all, and many will not come from homes that support the belief that education is important. Getting to know your students as individuals and knowing their strengths and weaknesses in learning mathematics will help you facilitate their learning.

The most important thing to remember is to take an interest in who your students are and value them for who they are. Make sure students know that they are valued, no matter what their cultural background, first language, gender, or strengths and weaknesses in mathematics. When your students come to feel a sense of belonging in their classroom, you will make great strides in creating a positive learning environment and, in addition, you will encourage engagement in learning mathematics.

STUDENTS ENGAGED IN LEARNING PROBABILITY

So far we have looked at important affective components in the mathematics classroom and what may be done to create a positive learning environment in your classroom. Next we will take a look at the behavioral and cognitive domains. We begin this discussion by looking at a fifth grade mathematics classroom that is studying probability. This vignette will help us to begin thinking about the different behavioral and cognitive components that help to make a lesson engaging.

Vignette 4: Fifth Grade Probability—Socializing by Spinners

Students in Mrs. Bermudez's fifth grade class have just finished up their language arts lesson for the day, and Mrs. Bermudez is transitioning into their mathematics lesson, a probability activity. The students in her fifth grade class have been placed at different lunch tables each week so that the students would get to know all of their fellow fifth graders in the school. She decides that she will share the "Sandy Hill Elementary School Secret" of how these seating assignments are selected. The students will be able to create the seating randomly themselves for the following week using the spinner "technology," as she refers to it. The students are very excited by this "secret." It also appears many are feeling empowered by using the technology the school used to select their seating. Each group is given a spinner that looks like this one:

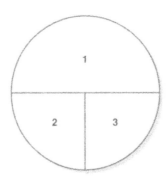

Mrs. Bermudez explains that they are going to use this spinner to break the class up into three different groups to determine at which table they will eat during lunch. The students who land on number 1 will have their own table, whereas those who land on numbers 2 and 3 will each have to share their table with part of another fifth grade class.

"Wow, that's a funny looking spinner," one student says as she looks at the spinner.

Mrs. Bermudez addresses the class after hearing this comment. "What do you notice about this spinner that is different from the other ones that we have worked with so far?"

One student responds, "This spinner looks bigger."

Another student says, "Well, the spinner is not really bigger, but number 1 is bigger."

"Yeah, they are not all the same size," adds another student.

Mrs. Bermudez refers them back to their handout. "I want each of you to think about how this spinner is different, and on your handout where you are asked for your prediction, write what you think will happen after spinning the spinner twenty times.

"Then I want you to gather in your groups and actually spin the spinner twenty times and record the results on a bar graph. Before you begin, you will need to decide which group member will take on each of the different roles of spinning the spinner, recording the data, and drawing the bar graph."

Eager to begin the task, the students quickly divvy up the specific roles and responsibilities as she requested.

As Mrs. Bermudez walks around the room, she observes students working and ensures that all groups have completed the first step of thinking about their prediction and writing it down. As soon as the predictions are recorded, students begin spinning the spinner and tallying the results. As the students complete the data collection phase, Mrs. Bermudez chooses one group to share their bar graphs on the board. After they have done so, Eric raises his hand and tells the class that his group got something different. Mrs. Bermudez takes this time to hear from all the groups about how their results turned out. She then uses this opportunity to show the class a simulation of the spinner activity using a graphing calculator on the overhead projector. She shows the class how the calculator could spin the spinner 200 times and produce a bar graph similar to what they had just done with twenty spins. The class discusses how the graphic display from the calculator compares with their own graphs.

Mrs. Bermudez points out that the more the spinner is spun, the closer the results become to what is expected mathematically, and she comments on the difference between experimental and theoretical probability. Although she does not use the term theoretical probability, *she asks the class to discuss what their predictions were and the mathematical reasoning behind their predictions. Students who correctly predicted that the spinner would land on number 1 more often than either number 2 or 3 have trouble explaining why. Mrs. Bermudez has them refer back to yesterday's activity, when the spinner looked like this:*

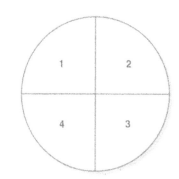

She asks, "What was the outcome of that experiment?"

One student responds, "All of the numbers were landed on about the same number of times. That's because they are all the same size."

Mrs. Bermudez asks, "If the whole circle represents 1, what is represented by each of the four portions?"

"One fourth," says the same student. "And that's the probability for landing on each number."

Mrs. Bermudez says, "Okay, now how can you use what you learned in yesterday's activity to help you come up with a reason why you would land more often on number 1 with today's spinner?" No one responds. Mrs. Bermudez suggests that they spend five minutes discussing this question in their groups and write down their answer on their handout. She is very aware of the importance of allowing wait time so that all students have time to process questions. As she walks around the room monitoring their conversations, comments such as, "Number 1 is bigger" are challenged by Mrs. Bermudez. "How much bigger?" she asks, until students come to realize that number 1 actually takes up half of the circle, whereas portions 2 and 3 each take up one-fourth of the circle.

Mrs. Bermudez then leads a discussion on the probability for landing on each region. She reminds them of the scenario of spinning for lunch tables: that twice as many students in their class will be chosen for table 1, because students at tables 2 and 3 will share half of their tables with another class. After the discussion, students are asked to predict how many times in forty spins the original spinner would land on numbers 1, 2, and 3 and to explain their reasoning in full sentences. They finish class time by actually assigning the fifth grade to seats in the lunchroom for the upcoming week.

For homework, Mrs. Bermudez asks her students to solve the following problems:

1. There are 64 students who need to be seated at three tables for lunch. (a) Predict the number of students who will be at each table. (b) Collect the data using the spinner used in class and record your results in a table. (c) Compare your prediction with the data from your experiment. Explain your answers using complete sentences.

2. Create a new spinner to assign students to four tables. You can make any type of spinner you like, but you will need to be able to determine the probability of landing on each table. When you are all finished with your spinners, you should color them and write the spinner question and answer on your paper. Explain your answers using complete sentences.

She follows up by stating, "I will choose several of the best papers to display on the mathematics wall in the classroom, so be sure to do your best work."

In this lesson, the fifth graders have been given a real-world problem-solving scenario that they can analyze using probability. Students have been asked to perform an experiment, make predictions about the expected outcomes, and provide mathematical justifications for the results. Included in this lesson are conceptual as well as procedural notions of probability, in addition to a distinction between experimental results and expected (theoretical) results based on mathematical principles.

Please note that this activity may be tailored for other grade levels. For example, this may easily be adapted for use in the sixth grade by asking the students to create their own, more challenging spinners. Sixth graders could be asked to create two different spinners, one that provides a high probability of their class all sitting together and one that provides a very low probability of the class sitting together. Students can include up to six lunch tables on their spinners, and the students can be asked to compute the probabilities for the spinners they have created.

Revisiting the Affective Domain

Before we discuss the behavioral and cognitive domains, let's briefly discuss the affective issues at play in this activity. We have purposefully chosen a basic lesson in probability to demonstrate that lessons do not all have to have the "wow" factor to be engaging. Teachers who are experienced in promoting a positive attitude in their students and encouraging their students to be active in their learning can take any lesson and make it engaging. Let's look at the specifics of what Mrs. Bermudez did to engage students in this lesson.

First, she began by involving all of the learners in a problem-solving lesson that contained information that was meaningful to them: where they sit at lunchtime. The students were intrigued and felt a sense of unity in learning the secret of the school lunch seating arrangements. By creating this scenario, Mrs. Bermudez helped to instill in her students a positive attitude toward learning mathematics. This set the tone for the affective factor related to engagement. She continued to intrigue her students by promising to put many of the spinners they created for homework on the mathematics wall, thus instilling in them a desire to do well as well as an interest in the spinners created by other classmates. Furthermore, Mrs. Bermudez treated all students with respect and entertained all questions in a nonjudgmental manner. It is obvious by observing just one lesson that her students admire her as their teacher and feel comfortable asking and answering questions as well as expressing any confusion they might be experiencing.

ENGAGING LEARNERS IN THE BEHAVIORAL DOMAIN

The primary format for traditional mathematics instruction has been the lecture. Typically, a teacher lectures on the topic of the day, shows the class several examples, and then the class practices the skills demonstrated in the lecture. In reform-based mathematics classrooms today, there is an increasing emphasis on interaction and student communication. These differences are reflected in the way the teacher presents material as well as the roles the students play in the class. In a lecture-style class, the student is responsible for little more than listening (and possibly taking notes) and practicing problems similar to the ones done on the board during the lecture. Further, the teacher is assumed to be the person who holds all the knowledge, and his or her job is to dispense it to the students.

In the probability vignette, Mrs. Bermudez's role in the classroom was a bit different than that of lecturer. She did not just present the lesson while her students watched; instead, she involved her students in the learning activity. She was more of a facilitator of learning than the sole holder of knowledge. In her role of facilitator, she promoted communication by her questioning techniques as well as her use of cooperative learning in the lesson. Note that Mrs. Bermudez was careful not to answer all questions posed to her without challenging her students to think more deeply. For example, when students were confused about why the spinner would land on number 1 more often than either numbers 2 or 3, she did not simply tell them the answer and proceed with the next item on her lesson plan. She allowed time for students to discuss their confusion and seek clarity on the issue before moving on. Mrs. Bermudez used questioning techniques to engage her students in constructing their own understanding.

Mrs. Bermudez also had her students work in groups to solve the problem. She created a structure for student mathematical communication and participation both within small groups and with a larger group. The act of grouping her students together during the problem-solving process encouraged students to interact with each other and to discuss the problem verbally. Cooperative learning (appropriately structured and implemented) is a good way to encourage mathematical discussions among classmates.

At the onset, it may be difficult to have your students work effectively in cooperative groups. However, with the help of a few techniques, this process can be improved. First, you must ensure that the activity you have selected is conducive to cooperative learning: activities that can be approached in a variety of ways or an experiment that involves more than one person to collect, record, and analyze the data. Keeping in mind what you know about your students, group them carefully, assign roles and responsibilities, use a self-evaluation tool for each student after each cooperative learning activity, and discuss appropriate participation.

One of the important features of cooperative learning is that every student needs to participate to make it successful. All students may not bring the same skills to the table, yet all students should participate at some level. In Mrs. Bermudez's probability lesson, there are roles for each member of the group that relate to spinning the spinners and recording and analyzing the data. A student who does not have mastery of basic probability is still able to participate in collecting and recording the data. He or she may need some assistance from the other group members to analyze the results, yet the student will have been able to fully participate up to that point and can take more of a learning role in the analysis phase.

When using cooperative learning regularly, it is important to discuss with your students effective ways to work in groups as well as how to speak appropriately in a respectful manner. For example, you may spend time role-playing using a mathematics problem. Ask a student to play the role of the teacher and to respond to you as if you were a student. In this role-playing experience, be sure to model correct student answers as well as partially correct and incorrect answers. Be sure to discuss the activity, specifically the responses of the teacher and how the students might like to be responded to if they were in that situation. This type of activity naturally can lead into a discussion about respect for each other and the teacher in the classroom.

When you are creating lessons for your students, behavioral components of engagement are important to consider. Cooperative learning is an extremely effective behavioral approach to engaging students, one that will reap rewards on the cognitive and affective levels as well. The more that your students actively participate in what they are learning, the more likely they are to remember the lesson and the more likely they will enjoy themselves and become engaged in learning mathematics.

ENGAGING LEARNERS IN THE COGNITIVE DOMAIN

As you may remember from our earlier discussion, the cognitive components in engagement relate to the mental effort and processing expended while learning something new. The quality of that mental effort involved in learning mathematics can be enriched in many ways. We begin by describing the use of multiple representations to engage learners using manipulatives. Manipulatives offer a means to represent mathematics more concretely. Subject-specific technology, such as graphing calculators and mathematics software, also serves to promote cognitive engagement in learning mathematics. We also focus on using problem solving to increase the mental effort students expend in their learning tasks.

Multiple Representations

Using multiple representations involves the presentation of a concept in different ways to promote understanding among more students. For example, when teaching a new concept, a teacher may use words, diagrams, pictures, equations, graphs, or symbolical representations. Students often need multiple methods of viewing a concept to understand it. Our discussion of Bruner's philosophy of learning in Chapter 2 focused on the idea that learners develop understanding of a concept by moving through three distinct modes of learning: concrete (hands-on), pictorial, and symbolic. As students develop their understanding of mathematics, their repertoire of representations increases and becomes more varied. For example, whereas students in Grades K–2 may use concrete representations, like blocks and pictures, to represent mathematics, students in Grades 3–6 may model mathematics using tables, graphs, and words in addition to concrete and pictorial models. If students are having difficulty with a concept, revisiting the concrete level may help facilitate their understanding.

You probably noticed in the vignette that Mrs. Bermudez incorporated multiple representations in her lesson on probability. Students were asked to represent their data in a bar graph, which provides a visual summary of the outcomes of the spinner. They also represented their data using words and numbers.

Manipulatives: These mathematical tools are a means to provide concrete explorations (the hands-on mode) for students in order to make mathematics more accessible in elementary school. Mrs. Bermudez provided students with a hands-on experience with probability experiments by allowing them to conduct an experiment with actual spinners. Most fifth graders are not ready to study probability at an abstract level, yet they can perform experiments and keep track of the outcomes. This manipulative allowed them to investigate probability at an appropriate level for them and created a foundation for more formal learning later.

Technology: Although some districts may not emphasize or require the use of technology in learning mathematics, it can be an integral part of a student's mathematical learning. Technology can be used to facilitate learning mathematics in a variety of ways: to demonstrate concepts visually, bring real-life data into the classroom, and engage learners in solving problems with actual data. Simple calculators can be used for developing number sense as well as for solving problems involving large numbers. Graphing calculators may be used in upper elementary grades to describe and analyze data using graphs and statistical calculations. Graphing calculators and other computer software may be used to simulate probability experiments. In addition, virtual manipulatives are available online for further enrichment of concepts learned with actual manipulatives in class.

The graphing calculator was used in the probability lesson as a tool to explore more repetitions of the experiment done by hand. This allows students whose data may not be representative of the theoretical probabilities to observe that larger data sets often more closely approximate theoretical outcomes.

Although there are many benefits to using technology as an instructional tool, the technology itself can be a more abstract representation than using concrete objects to develop a mathematical concept. This is especially true for younger students, so we suggest that, when including technology in your lessons, you seek a balance between different levels of abstraction. It is important to remember that technology should be used as an instructional

Benefits of Technology for Students

- Visually demonstrates concepts
- Brings real-life data into the classroom
- Engages learners

tool to increase students' understanding of mathematics and not just for the sake of using technology. And using technology allows you to easily demonstrate concepts in a visual manner and engage learners, which can help reach a wider range of students.

Problem Solving

Another strategy to support student engagement in the cognitive domain is problem solving. In the probability vignette, Mrs. Bermudez created an interesting problem-solving situation for her learners by asking them to investigate how the lunchtime seating could be determined for their grade. Students who are learning interesting mathematics and are continually challenged to the peak of their ability levels are more likely to thrive in the classroom.

Mathematically speaking, students need to be exposed to both conceptual and procedural understandings, and they can benefit at all levels from seeing mathematics as a connected body of knowledge. Incorporating the use of problem solving in your lessons will allow you to challenge more students on different cognitive levels. It is good to remember that problem solving can range from simple word problems to complex, open-ended tasks. Problem solving is an experience, unlike solving exercises: Typically students have not solved the types of problems given to them in problem-solving scenarios. In addition, if the problem solving is within a meaningful context, it will be more engaging to the learner. For instance, see the next problem-solving scenario, from the National Council of Teachers of Mathematics (2007):

The Mangoes Problem

One night the King couldn't sleep, so he went down into the royal kitchen, where he found a bowl full of mangoes. Being hungry, he took $\frac{1}{6}$ of the mangoes. Later that same night, the Queen was hungry and couldn't sleep. She, too, found the mangoes and took $\frac{1}{5}$ of what the King had left. Still later, the first Prince awoke, went to the kitchen, and ate $\frac{1}{4}$ of the remaining mangoes. Even later, his brother, the second Prince, ate $\frac{1}{3}$ of what was then left. Finally, the third Prince ate $\frac{1}{2}$ of what was left, leaving only three mangoes for the servants. How many mangoes were originally in the bowl?

This problem enables students to approach learning on a variety of levels, depending on their level of current understanding. There are numerous approaches a student could take to solve this problem, which makes it accessible to students with a broad range of ability levels. Students could try to solve the problem by guessing and checking, for example. They could also use a picture or pattern blocks to represent the initial quantity and continue to divide the picture or blocks into the appropriate fractional parts. Students could solve this problem by working backwards. Because they know that three mangoes remained at the end, they could work backwards at each step to determine how many mangoes there were previously. Finally, students could solve this problem using an equation for each of the stages of removing mangoes.

This problem can be changed to make it more meaningful for the students based on the season or current events. For example, if this problem were done around Thanksgiving, a farmer could take turkeys instead of mangoes, or at Easter, the bunny could take eggs.

Bloom's taxonomy is one well-known classification scheme that describes a hierarchy of six levels of cognitive objectives: knowledge, comprehension, application, analysis, synthesis, and evaluation. In most textbooks, there are plenty of knowledge, comprehension, and, to a lesser extent, application problems. It is harder to find rich problems that challenge students to perform at the three higher levels, analysis, synthesis, and evaluation. Providing rich problems gives students opportunities to analyze the problem situation, evaluate which method will work best for them, and synthesize the information they get at each step of the problem.

The key to cognitive engagement is to use methods that promote deeper thinking about the mathematical topics they are learning. Rather than leading students toward solving their problems in one particular way or presenting problems in only one format, it is more effective to teach students general problem-solving skills and to use multiple representations of mathematical concepts and content. These teaching methods create a cognitively richer experience that can engage your students and ultimately help them succeed in mathematics.

SUMMARY

In this chapter, we focused on the three components of engagement: affective, behavioral, and cognitive. Although we looked at each factor separately, it is important to realize that all of these components are intertwined. Students who are engaged cognitively at the appropriate level have more opportunities for success in mathematics, thus improving their attitude toward the subject. In turn, active engagement in communication about mathematics tends to influence understanding as well. Paying attention to each factor will serve you well in creating a positive classroom environment.

Engagement Strategies for Special Populations

In Chapter 3 we discussed three components of engagement: affective, behavioral, and cognitive. These issues and their strategies are often intertwined. In this chapter, we present strategies for three special populations: gifted, special needs, and English language learners. As you read, you will probably be able to identify the affective, behavioral, or cognitive components, although they are not delineated.

THE SPECIAL NEEDS LEARNER

Know Your Learner

In this book, the term *special needs learner* refers to students who have been identified as having learning disabilities. These students fall across a spectrum; are unique; and have their own defining affective, cognitive, and behavioral characteristics. When planning instruction to include a student with special learning needs, it helps to have an understanding of the student's attributes that challenge or interfere with learning. As well as speaking with previous mathematics teachers, you may want to speak with other professionals who have had contact with your special needs students in the past, such as psychologists or special education teachers. In addition, documents from these professionals, such as individualized education plans (IEPs), will also provide useful information.

Create a Positive Classroom Culture

Creating a positive classroom culture supports engagement and the learning of mathematics for all students. The most important aspect here is the belief that the student can and will be successful in mathematics. Without this belief, the student is much less likely to succeed. Research has found that the teacher is the single most important variable in the success of a student (Sliva & Roddick, 2001). It is very important that the teacher not create low expectations for achievement for any student, especially those who have a history of mathematical difficulties, such as students who struggle and students labeled as having special needs on the basis of an IEP or prior experiences a teacher has had with the student. Often these students have had learning experiences in which they have been taught using an inferior curriculum, thereby not being given the same opportunities as their peers who do not have learning disabilities. Lower expectations cheat these students of opportunities to learn. A strong belief that the student can and will learn mathematics can be the single most important aspect of teaching these students.

We have previously addressed the importance of maintaining high standards for all learners. This is critical for special needs learners. It is crucial that teachers establish and maintain high expectations for these learners, as traditionally their instruction lacks content and depth in relation to the instruction of their peers without learning disabilities. Typically, these students have experienced failure in the classroom. Because of this, they are often placed in skills-based classrooms and, as a result, many of these students never experience a conceptually higher level of mathematics and are left out of reform-based mathematics (Baxter, Woodward, & Olson, 2001). Thus they are not provided with the same opportunities nor expected to participate in activities with their peers, often leading to a lack of engagement. One important guiding principle when engaging these learners is to expect all students to learn both concepts and skills and not to limit any student to just skill-based learning. Expect high-level products and high-level thinking (e.g., writing, proofs, projects, solutions to challenging problems). Without high expectations and high standards for all students, there may be equity issues felt by all learners, which may not contribute to a positive classroom culture.

An additional characteristic of special needs students that can impact their ability to learn mathematics is difficulty maintaining a positive attitude (Sliva, 2003). Many special needs students have had failure throughout their experiences learning mathematics and often think they "cannot do mathematics."

As a reminder, the following strategies mentioned in Chapter 3 are helpful with special needs students as well:

- Make learning meaningful.
- Model enthusiasm toward learning and doing mathematics.
- Require students to write about their attitudes and feelings toward learning mathematics.
- Provide the opportunity for students to demonstrate for other students what they have learned, and teach them to compliment one another for trying hard and being successful.
- Deemphasize goals that foster competition among students.

Increase Opportunities for Communication and Participation

In the probability vignette from Chapter 3, it's likely that you noticed there were a variety of instructional materials and methods used to include all learners. Special needs students' specific needs were addressed by using strategic groupings and multiple avenues to see the mathematics in different ways. Mrs. Bermudez used various teaching techniques, such as active participation in data collection, visual representation of the data in a bar graph, and verbal discussion of the results and reasoning related to the experiment. This example illuminates our suggestions for increasing communication and participation:

- Use cooperative groupings (with appropriate placement and structures).
- Allow alternative methods to express mathematical ideas.

Research has found that many special needs students have difficulties in the area of language, both with processing and understanding and with expression. Both of these areas may impact a student's participation in class. As demonstrated in the vignette, small-group work, including cooperative learning, has been shown to be effective when engaging these learners. These students will often need encouragement to participate in their learning. Be sure to carefully group students with others who are sensitive to the students' special needs in the areas of communication. In addition, a structure for how students will participate that includes expectations for respect, responsibilities, and communication strategies within groups must also be established. Students with special needs may participate in varying ways; this is to be expected. However, it must be assumed that they will all participate!

By allowing students to use alternative methods to express their thinking, you may be able to obtain more information about their mathematical understandings. Students may use manipulatives or pictorial representations to express their thinking in large or small groups or even as a one-on-one assessment. In addition, some students may express themselves better verbally than when using a paper and pencil. This is especially true for students who may have visual-processing or motor-processing difficulties. As a teacher it is important to be aware that these students may take longer to respond and need more wait time in the classroom than the other students.

As with all students, learning about the areas of strength and weakness for special needs students is very important because a teacher will want to teach to a students' strength to address their weakness. For example, if a student has relative strengths in taking in information visually and relative weaknesses receiving information verbally, the teacher will want to represent mathematics visually as well as verbally as much as possible. This will enable the student to increase his or her mathematical knowledge by taking in the information in their strength as well as work on strengthening the verbal avenue of receiving information.

Differentiate Instructional Strategies

As we mentioned, traditional instruction was led by the teacher and "given" to a group of students. Often this instruction was not flexible for the wide range of learners in the classroom. Differentiation of teaching strategies allows the same high-quality instruction to reach all learners, and this instruction is tailored to reach a large spectrum. Teachers may differentiate teaching strategies on the basis of the information gathered and synthesized in the process of knowing their students. This may sound like creating 30 different lesson plans for 30 different students; it need not be true. A few easy strategies can help meet the needs of many students.

To begin the process, we suggest gathering the following additional information for these students:

- How does the student learn mathematics best? Do they prefer to use hands-on manipulatives or to draw their ideas?
- How much prerequisite mathematics content has the student mastered? For example, if the student is going into third grade, prerequisite knowledge may include mastery of the concept of equal parts; recognizing unit fractions, such as $\frac{1}{2}$, $\frac{1}{3}$, or $\frac{1}{4}$; or solving problems using addition and subtraction.

Here are a few suggestions for how to differentiate instruction in the mathematics classroom:

- Present new concepts using Bruner's model (as discussed in Chapter 2) using in turn (1) concrete manipulatives, (2) pictures, and

(3) numbers or symbols. This research-based sequence of instruction engages learners in a new concept at a concrete level and then progresses to a more abstract level. Special needs students may need varying amounts of time at each of the first couple of levels.

- Use a think-aloud strategy that enables the teacher to model appropriate behaviors. A teacher that models personal thinking processes and strategies for solving a problem out loud is using the think-aloud strategy.
- Create a template to isolate information: To remove distractions, create window templates to isolate certain problems, paragraphs, or sentences on a page. The templates may be created on a computer, and students can keep templates in their notebooks for use when needed.

Cognitive research on teaching and learning emphasizes the importance of making connections. Hiebert and Carpenter (1992) state that the degree of a student's understanding is determined by the number, accuracy, and strength of connections. For example, it is useful for students to understand the inverse relationship between multiplication and division, as the concept is used when developing rules for integer operations and for solving equations. Many students with special needs have difficulty making connections when learning mathematics content. Here are a few strategies for helping these students gain this skill:

- Use concept maps: A concept map ties newly learned concepts to other mathematical ideas. As students create concept maps, they visually illustrate mathematical connections and describe them in writing.
- Use graphic organizers: A graphic organizer helps students see patterns within mathematical ideas and generalize them. Graphic organizers also reduce the demand on language.
- Make connections to other curricular areas: When students interact with mathematics in other disciplines, it can help to strengthen and generalize their understanding of the mathematics. (Chapter 6 contains examples of making connections to other content areas.)

Keep in mind that all students learn at different paces and in different ways, and special needs students are especially vulnerable to pacing issues. Be flexible in your expectations about pacing for different students. Whereas some students may be mastering basic skills, others may be working on more advanced problems. For example, in the elementary grades, although learners still need to know their basic facts, do not hold these students back from other, more complex tasks. Rather, continue to work in parallel on the basic facts.

There are many students with special learning needs who may not be identified as such in a school district and therefore may not be eligible for special services. As you learn about all of your students, you may find strategies for your identified students that may also be useful for the rest of your students.

To learn more details and specific information about teaching mathematics to students with special needs, see *Teaching Inclusive Mathematics to Special Learners, K–6*, by Julie A. Sliva (2003).

THE GIFTED LEARNER

Know Your Learner

Gifted students come from all ethnic and socioeconomic groups, are both male and female, and may not demonstrate their gifts in all content areas. Gifted students demonstrate their talent in mathematics in a range of ways and at varying points in their development. They may differ from their peers by the pace at which they learn. Many gifted learners respond favorably to challenge and have the need for continual intellectual stimulation. The teacher should be careful not to stifle their curiosity or make them feel as if they are a burden because they have different needs. They differ in the depth of their understanding of mathematics; deeper levels of understanding and abstraction are possible for most mathematical topics, so differentiation becomes important. Knowing your gifted students' areas of strength and weakness can help you better tailor their mathematics instruction. In addition to contacting your students' previous teachers and obtaining prior relevant documents, it is wise to seek out any other professionals, such as specialists for gifted learners and counselors in the school, who may have dealt specifically with the student around these issues.

Similar to special needs students, these students may not be identified as gifted. It is crucial to spot such giftedness early because if it isn't encouraged, it may never develop. Students who are gifted in mathematics are likely to demonstrate the ability to

- learn and understand mathematical ideas quickly;
- be analytical, think logically, and easily see mathematical relationships;
- learn and process complex information very rapidly;
- identify patterns and make connections between concepts easily;
- easily apply their knowledge in new or unfamiliar contexts;
- communicate their reasoning and justify their methods;

- ask questions that show clear understanding of, and curiosity about, mathematics;
- take a creative approach to solving mathematical problems;
- sustain their concentration throughout longer tasks and persist in seeking solutions; and
- be more adept at posing their own questions and pursuing lines of inquiry (Maker, 1982).

Create a Positive Classroom Culture

There are affective issues specific to gifted learners that need to be addressed. The National Association for Gifted Children (NAGC) includes an affective component to their gifted program standards. They suggest that gifted learners be provided with affective curriculum in addition to other services:

Gifted learners who are comfortable with their abilities are more likely to use their talents in positive ways. High-ability students need specific curriculum that addresses their socio-emotional needs and enhances development of the whole child, rather than just focusing on cognitive development. (NAGC, 2005)

They suggest that gifted learners realize they are different from their peers but have no outlet to discuss these differences and may interpret this difference negatively unless they have assistance in accepting such strengths. Obtaining support for your students from gifted professionals and counselors knowledgeable in this area is suggested. Overall, it is important that these students realize that you value their abilities and encourage their curiosity. It is important to encourage students in their mathematical strengths and not turn them away from mathematics at a young age.

Increase Opportunities for Communication and Participation

It is interesting that promoting communication with gifted learners can also have challenges. Unlike their special needs and English language learner peers, they may obtain information much more quickly, process it more quickly, and as a result want to "go it alone." This can lead to isolation from their peers and from the benefits of working collaboratively in groups. These benefits may include practicing social, communication, and perhaps leadership skills.

Ideally, in cooperative groupings, all gifted students would learn at or near the pace of the quickest pupil, and this would be combined with plenty of communication among group members to sharpen their social abilities. However, this is not always practical, and in many heterogeneous classrooms it can seem like an unlikely scenario. Providing structured groupings with tasks assigned to each member can support more communication for these learners. In addition, it may be important to speak with parents of these students to explain the benefits of group work for their child. Often parents of gifted children will feel that their child is being held back from learning to their fullest potential because they are with "slower" learners. However, they are often unaware of the other benefits of cooperative grouping, such as the development of social, communication, and leadership skills. Be sure to ensure that these students are not perceived as the "teacher" or that they are always responsible for helping out the "slower" students.

Differentiate Instructional Strategies

A dilemma facing many mathematics teachers every day is how to make available mathematical opportunities that encourage advanced pursuits of excellence without denying other students access to high-quality mathematics. We need to provide high-level instruction for all learners, including gifted students. Typically, gifted students are given more work than the rest of the students. For example, if the students are assigned problems 1–25, the gifted students may be given problems 1–35. This is not always an effective way to engage these students; gifted students should do more challenging problems, not just more problems. It is important to note that a gifted program is not synonymous with acceleration. Gifted students need to be encouraged to learn the concepts of their grade level more deeply, in addition to furthering their knowledge.

To meet their needs and engage these students, there are several areas in which a teacher may differentiate instruction: content, allowing for student preferences, altering the pace of instruction, creating a flexible classroom environment, and using specific instructional strategies. According to Johnson (1993), components of mathematics curriculum for the gifted are as follows:

- Content with greater depth and higher levels of complexity
- A discovery approach that encourages students to explore concepts
- A focus on solving complex, open-ended problems
- Opportunities for interdisciplinary connections

The following are strategies that may be used to differentiate instruction for gifted learners in the mathematics classroom (Johnson, 2000):

- Give preassessments so that students who already know the material do not have to repeat it but may be provided with instruction and activities that are meaningful. These assessments should be given so that students may be able to express their understanding both orally and in writing.
- Choose textbooks that provide enrichment opportunities. Unfortunately, because most curricula in this country are determined by the textbooks used and these textbooks are written expressly for the average population, they are not always appropriate for the gifted. No single text will adequately meet the needs of these learners; therefore, teachers need to supplement with multiple resources.
- Use inquiry-based, discovery learning approaches that emphasize open-ended problems with multiple solutions or multiple paths to solutions. Allow students to design their own ways to find the answers to complex questions. More information on this topic can be found in the assessment chapter (Chapter 5).
- Use lots of higher-level questions in justification and discussion of problems. Ask "why" and "what if" questions.
- Provide units, activities, or problems that extend beyond the normal curriculum. Offer challenging mathematical recreation, such as puzzles and games.
- Differentiate assignments. It is not appropriate to give more problems of the same type to gifted students. You might give students a choice of a regular assignment; a different, more challenging one; or a task that is tailored to specific interests.
- Provide opportunities to participate in contests such as Mathematical Olympiads.
- Bring a variety of speakers into the classroom to explain how mathematics has opened doors in their professions and careers.
- Provide some activities that can be done independently or in groups on the basis of student choice. Be careful to provide appropriate instruction for these students and not just let them work on their own, as they too need instruction.
- Provide useful concrete experiences. Even though gifted learners may be capable of abstraction and may move from concrete to abstract more rapidly, they still benefit from the use of manipulatives and hands-on activities.

Possible Pitfalls

Gifted children think and learn differently from other students. Asking them to serve as tutors could be a frustrating experience for all parties involved. Therefore, it is important to carefully consider the pairings of students and how each may feel about tutoring. This should also be a consideration when putting together learning teams or group projects.

Because these students seem to finish the work in a more efficient manner than their peers, it is counterproductive to give them more of the same assignment. This is an excellent opportunity for students to work on challenge problems. It is important to provide parallel work that is challenging for the student and not just more of the same work. It is important to remember that gifted students process information differently, and it is imperative that you focus on their strengths, not their shortcomings. Offer them opportunities that are consistent with their abilities.

THE ENGLISH LANGUAGE LEARNER

Know Your Learner

Similar to other special populations of students, these students have a wide range of diversity in their needs as they often have a great deal of variability in their backgrounds and thus need different pathways for their success. Research has found that it may take as long as seven years to acquire a level of language proficiency comparable to native speakers (Collier, 1989). The result is that the majority of language minority students do not have access to rigorous subject matter instruction or the opportunity to develop an academic language—the language functions and structures that are needed to understand, conceptualize, symbolize, discuss, read, and write about topics in academic subjects (LaCelle-Peterson & Rivera, 1994). Therefore, it is essential that you learn as much as possible about the previous experiences and backgrounds of your English language learners (ELLs) to engage them and facilitate their learning of mathematics. In addition to their content area knowledge and experiences in learning mathematics, understanding their cultural norms and background are essential to effectively teach them. As is the case for all students, the parents or guardians are rich sources of information, especially in the area of cultural understandings.

Specific information you may want to learn about your students:

- What language do they prefer to use when discussing mathematics?
- How well does the student work individually, in small groups, cooperative environments, or a large group setting?

You may also want to collaborate with other professionals who have experience working with English language learners. As a new teacher of mathematics, working closely with the professional in your school or district responsible for these students can be invaluable. This professional may be called an English as a Second Language teacher (or an ESL teacher). These individuals should have different and more in-depth knowledge about the student and about teaching English language learners in general. Other professionals in the building that are also teaching the student will also be useful as they may have learned or know of strategies that will work to reach these students.

Create a Positive Classroom Culture

As with the other two populations we have discussed, creating a positive classroom culture is important to engage ELLs in learning mathematics. These learners are also often excluded from high expectations as it may be difficult to determine their mathematical backgrounds because of language barriers, and it may be assumed that, like their limited English proficiency, their mathematics skills are limited. In addition, those students who have mathematics skills that may exceed your average students need an environment in which their abilities are valued and supported for further growth. Challenging, age-appropriate lessons provide opportunities for these students.

Second-language acquisition theories address cognitive, affective, and linguistic issues. Affective filters in individuals (created by a variety of factors, such as motivation, self-confidence, or anxiety) can support or disrupt acquisition of a second language (Brown, 2001). To positively impact these affective issues and thus engage learners in the mathematics classroom, you can do the following:

- Create a classroom environment in which learners feel comfortable using and taking risks with English. Incorporate cooperative learning activities that facilitate the building of a positive classroom community. Be sure to integrate your English-speaking and ELLs in group activities.
- Promote a low-stress classroom culture. It is critical that a mathematics classroom for ELLs be as stress-free as possible. Students need to feel comfortable making mistakes, in both their usage of English and mathematics, so that they may develop their mathematical thinking. Avoid constant error correction and include activities that focus on overall ability to communicate meaning.

Increase Opportunities for Communication and Participation

ELLs are at a disadvantage from their English-speaking peers in the mathematics classroom. Not having the command of the English language that native speakers do, they may take longer to understand what is asked of them. The following are strategies for helping these students communicate their mathematical ideas in English and to better support their thinking of different strategies for solving problems (Bresser, 2003):

• *Modify the way you talk.* Specifically, when you are speaking to a class with ELLs, you should speak slowly and use clear articulation. Build in instructional strategies that focus more on demonstration than language to support the understanding of new concepts and terms. Be sure to stress important words, exaggerate intonation, and use simple words to describe a concept. Be aware of the terms you are using, including any new vocabulary necessary for understanding the lesson. For example, when teaching a concept such as fractions, present a visual representation, such as pictures. In addition, you will want to include as many opportunities as possible for students to communicate mathematically both with the teacher and with each other so as to engage them.

• *Ask questions and use prompts.* For example, what do you think the answer will be? Why do you think that? Can you explain to me how you found your answer? How did you begin the problem? What did you do first? Then what did you do? Can you tell me what the problem is saying in your own words?

• *Practice wait time.* After you have asked a question, allow sufficient time before you ask a specific student to answer. This will enable all learners, especially ELLs, time to think about the question you are asking, formulate an answer, and respond.

• *Appropriately state mathematical ideas and concepts in language.* As mentioned previously, it is essential to use correct terminology. For example, when teaching about the concept of addition, be sure to use other terms that represent addition, such as *sum.* However, one line of caution: Too many terms can often confuse a student when learning a new concept.

• *Connect symbols with words.* Whenever possible, point to the symbols, such as =, >, and <, when you are discussing them. This provides one more possibility for students to strengthen their knowledge and understanding of the symbols and their meaning.

• *Use "Think-Pair-Share."* This strategy works well when students are asked to share with a partner, discuss the idea, and then share with the group. With the first step of sharing with a partner, the students are practicing formulating their mathematical thinking as well as their expression of the idea in English, which enables them to alter what they are thinking or saying prior to expressing it to an entire group.

• *Use "English experts."* Using this strategy, students explain their thinking in their own language to a more capable English speaker and then the "English expert" translates the ideas for the teacher. Again, this enables the ELL to practice communication in the classroom with the support of a student who can assist in the translation. Thus, these students are not left out of a discussion.

• *Encourage students to retell.* This strategy enables the student to focus on their communication in English primarily and the mathematics secondarily. Students are asked to restate and explain, sometimes elaborating on a strategy another student in their group may have used.

• *Use the buddy system.* Allow students with limited English proficiency to bring an English-speaking peer to the board to support an explanation of a problem.

Think back to Mr. Callahan's lesson on fractions discussed in Chapter 1. He was very concerned that all of his students have equal access to participation in his class; therefore, he allowed all students to take a peer to the board to assist in explaining the problem. Please note: Not only ELLs may have difficulties explaining or expressing their thoughts; so may other students. Use of manipulatives on the overhead or in small-group situations may also be of assistance for students with these challenges.

It is important to note that although many of these strategies are particularly appropriate for ELLs, they are also useful to increase mathematical communication with all students in your classroom.

Differentiate Instructional Strategies

When teaching a mathematics lesson to ELLs, it is important to build in instructional strategies that focus on demonstration to support the understanding of new concepts and terms. The following is a list of cognitive strategies that may be used to engage students:

• Pose problems in a familiar context. As we mentioned previously, problem solving challenges your learners on many different levels. With a familiarity of structure, the student can more easily focus on how to solve the problem rather than on other obstacles that may interfere with their ability to learn mathematics.

- Integrate ELLs' culture into lessons whenever possible. Give students opportunities to share examples from schools in their home countries and different ways of learning mathematics.
- Make interdisciplinary connections whenever possible and tap prior knowledge. Connect students' prior knowledge and experiences to new learning. Find out what students already know about a topic by making a concept map on the board. For example, when beginning to teach fractions, one might want to see how much prerequisite knowledge the student has with regard to related concepts, such as the sharing model of division. This related knowledge can be linked to the concept of fractions by the use of a concept map.

Once again, engagement is an important issue to keep in the forefront of your mind as you teach. The three areas—affective, behavioral, and cognitive—are interrelated in many ways, and all contribute to the engagement of your students in your classroom. An activity follows that embodies the aspects we have discussed with regard to engagement.

EXAMPLE OF ENGAGING LEARNERS IN A MATHEMATICS CLASSROOM

Tessellations and Geometry

The study of tessellations is an engaging example connecting mathematics and art. *Tessellation* means covering a plane without gaps or overlaps with the use of geometric figures, similar to creating a mosaic. This series of activities involves students collaboratively investigating which regular polygons tessellate a plane and the connections between the measurements of the interior angles. The NCTM (2000) *Principles and Standards* document recommends that geometry be learned using concrete models, drawings, and dynamic software.

Have students begin this investigation by giving each of them a card stock cutout of two shapes that tessellate, such as a square and an equilateral triangle or hexagon. The goals of this part of the activity are that students (a) investigate different regular polygons and determine which tessellate and then (b) create a template of a figure that, when repeated, creates a tessellation that can cover an entire page without overlapping. This tessellation template should be created by having students use the movements of rotation (turn), translation (slide or glide), and reflection (flip). See Figure 4.1 for an example. The students should be given time to collaboratively investigate each of these movements before they decide which one(s) they may use to create their own tessellation. Once the students have created their templates and used them to create their tessellations, they may color and display their final pieces of artwork for possible display in the classroom.

Figure 4.1   Creating a tessellation by translation (slide)

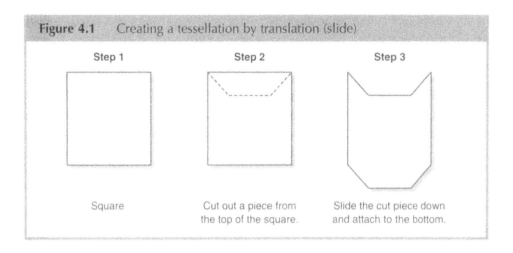

Step 1	Step 2	Step 3
Square	Cut out a piece from the top of the square.	Slide the cut piece down and attach to the bottom.

After the students have completed the hands-on activity of tiling the plane, they may continue to collaboratively investigate tessellations by inspecting different regular polygons to determine which of these tessellate a plane and why. Students can then use the measurement of the interior angles to decide whether or not a regular polygon will tessellate. They can use pattern blocks and other regular polygons cut out of paper as a hands-on investigation. To challenge the students who may have easily understood the previous concepts, have them delve deeper into the study of tessellations by investigating nonregular polygons. For example, a regular pentagon does *not* tessellate, but many nonregular pentagons will.

Next, the students may use a computer software program to create their own tessellations and investigate the mathematics further, as well as learn a bit of the historical background of tessellations. Students could be expected to share their newly acquired understandings with their groups and the entire class. In addition, students may investigate the connections to art and the history of tessellations by looking at, for example, the work of M. C. Escher or the tiles in the Alhambra in Spain.

Please note: Students may also use the draw capability in Microsoft Word to complete a tessellation if tessellation software is not available in the school.

Discussion

These tessellation activities may be adapted for a variety of elementary grade levels to investigate tessellations and the ties to history and art, as well as the mathematics involved. In these activities, you will notice some of Glasser's ideas. Students are engaged in the learning process by using concrete manipulatives to facilitate their learning. They are also connecting mathematics to art. This adds a *fun* element to the mathematics classroom because students are discovering and creating their own understanding of mathematics rather than merely being told what they are supposed to be learning. A teacher creates a *sense of belonging* in the classroom by recognizing individual students' efforts and their work. Students can display their creations on the wall, developing a sense of belonging in the classroom because they have contributed to decorating it. This is particularly good for some students who may not always get an "A" paper and have it displayed; this type of activity tends to level the playing field, as all may complete an activity that is decorative, using either their hand-created tessellation or one created using a computer. A sense of belonging can be fostered by creating an atmosphere of learning where everyone can participate at some level. Another way is by acknowledging and encouraging students for their efforts. A sense of *freedom* can be promoted by allowing students to make choices regarding their learning. In the examples, students were allowed to create the template that they would be tessellating. Finally, *power* is instilled throughout by having students explain their understandings to the rest of the class and by displaying students' quality work.

Each of Glasser's Five Basic Needs contributes in a significant way to the development of a lesson that addresses each of the affective, behavioral, and cognitive factors. Students are engaged affectively when the lesson is interesting and provides attainable levels of success so that they develop a positive attitude toward learning mathematics. Students are engaged behaviorally by the interactive design of the activity, necessitating participation and communication. Finally, by investigating the interior angles of different regular polygons, students are required to reason about why a particular polygon tessellates, which speaks to the cognitive factor of engagement.

The design of this activity is also inclusive for special needs students. Research suggests that special needs students benefit from using hands-on manipulatives to facilitate understanding of mathematical concepts. Students such as ELLs, special needs students, and low achievers have more opportunities for success, because they can be cognitively engaged at an appropriate level. The activity includes elements from all three of Bruner's stages: concrete, pictorial, and symbolic, thus providing elements of mathematics at several different levels.

SUMMARY

At this point, we hope you have begun to consider how your philosophy of teaching mathematics becomes intertwined with your philosophy of classroom engagement. Carefully planning your lessons to include the best practices from Chapter 1, ideas from the principles and standards in Chapter 2, and the key elements of engagement (affective, behavioral, and cognitive) discussed in Chapter 3, will provide you with tools to successfully engage your students in learning mathematics.

Again let us emphasize that engagement issues are intertwined. Although we have separated out the issues for discussion purposes and have even addressed certain pieces of the vignettes as affective, behavioral, or cognitive, each of these impact the other. For example, in the probability vignette in Chapter 3, although we refer to using the spinner as a cognitive strategy for engaging learners, it also impacts both behavioral and affective domains. Students were engaged at the concrete level, which enabled them to communicate their learning and become a part of the learning community. Therefore, there is an interrelatedness and importance of focusing on all three domains when teaching mathematics. As you focus on each of these domains in your teaching, you will begin to notice an increase in your students' engagement and knowledge of mathematics.

The following is a summary of engagement strategies to address the special populations we discussed in this chapter.

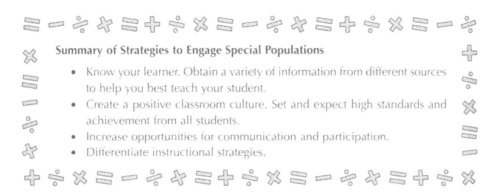

Summary of Strategies to Engage Special Populations

- Know your learner. Obtain a variety of information from different sources to help you best teach your student.
- Create a positive classroom culture. Set and expect high standards and achievement from all students.
- Increase opportunities for communication and participation.
- Differentiate instructional strategies.

5 Assessment

ssessment is a key component in helping you teach all of your learners, a tool to help you determine whether your methods of instruction are successful. According to the NCTM (1995), there are four major purposes for assessment: (1) monitoring student progress, (2) making instructional decisions, (3) evaluating student achievement, and (4) evaluating programs. You can see that in addition to being used to evaluate students for grades, assessment can inform and shape lessons as it sheds light on what does and does not work for particular students. Keeping with the focus on diverse learners, we present several different strategies for assessing understanding and for assessing special needs populations. As you read through this chapter, be sure to keep all learners in mind, including the ones you read about in Chapter 4.

As you begin your teaching career, you must consider many aspects of assessment that will guide your philosophy of teaching. In this chapter we discuss how to develop different types of assessments and the use of rubrics, and we demonstrate how to change a traditional assessment item into a variety of different nontraditional assessments for an elementary classroom. Adaptations for special populations are also discussed.

DEVELOPING ASSESSMENTS: THE USE OF BACKWARD DESIGN

All too often, assessment is the last thing considered when planning a lesson. The teacher plans the lesson, teaches it, and then, often as an afterthought, decides on an assessment, picking out problems that seem to address the main ideas or simply using the assessments supplied with the book. The use of *backward design* ensures that assessment is among the *first* things a teacher considers when designing a lesson. According to Wiggins and McTighe (1998),

> Rather than creating assessments near the conclusion of a unit of study (or relying on the tests provided by textbook publishers, which may not completely or appropriately assess our standards), backward design calls for us to operationalize our goals or our standards in terms of assessment evidence as we begin to plan a unit or a course. (p. 8)

This process forces teachers to think about how they are going to assess what they want students to know before they begin instruction, which often clarifies the goals for instruction.

Stages of Backward Design

There are three stages involved in the process of backward design. After each is discussed, an example is provided to help you understand the simplicity and necessity for this process in assessment.

Stage 1: Identify Desired Results

The first step is to determine the standards (district, state, and/or NCTM) that you will address for the lesson or unit. Then consider the topics, skills, and resources that need to be examined. Next, important knowledge (such as facts, concepts, and principles) as well as skills (processes, strategies, and methods) should be considered. Finally, look at the enduring understandings that anchor the unit, the *big ideas*. All of these big ideas should be delineated at this time.

For example, if you want to focus on the major goal of developing an understanding of geometry, you must first select the standards that you wish to address. Let's look at one of NCTM's Standards for Geometry in Grades PreK–2: "Recognize, name, build, draw, compare, and sort two- and three-dimensional shapes." Specific skills and concepts we want students to acquire are to recognize, name, and describe several attributes of a square, triangle, and hexagon. Students should know the number of sides and angles for each figure and be able to draw each figure. For example, kindergarten students can be asked to pick out a square, triangle, and hexagon from a group of objects.

Stage 2: Determine Acceptable Evidence

The big question that we consider here is, "How will you determine whether your students have achieved the desired results?" Wiggins and

McTighe (1998) suggest a variety of assessment methods that include informal checks for understanding, observations and dialogue, quizzes and tests, open-ended prompts, and performance tasks and projects. The most important piece at this stage is to determine the methods you will use to assess your students.

Using the PreK–2 standard for geometry that we looked at in Stage 1, we can think about how to assess understanding throughout the instructional activities. One example could be to require the students to sort several two- and three-dimensional figures and to identify them by their names. More advanced students could also be required to draw a picture of each of the figures and to label the number of sides and angles.

Stage 3: Plan Learning Experiences

Once you have determined the desired outcomes and created or selected appropriate ways for learning to be assessed, you are now ready to plan instructional activities. For example, at the kindergarten level, students are given a group of two- or three-dimensional figures (or a combination of both) and required to sort them into separate piles. The Train Game, using attribute blocks, is also an appropriate activity to develop students' understanding of the standard. To play the Train Game, students have a rule, such as "one attribute must be different," that they must follow as they place their blocks down on the table in a "train." For example, if a student chooses a small, thin, red circle, the next student would have to choose a block with only one attribute different from the previous student's block, such as a large, thin, red, circle.

Three Stages of Backward Design

Stage 1: Identify desired results

Stage 2: Determine acceptable evidence

Stage 3: Plan learning experiences

TYPES OF ASSESSMENT

NCTM (2001) describes several types of assessment, which range from traditional unit tests or quizzes to open-ended projects. In this section, we develop an item representative of each of the different types of assessment. We have selected the topic of area and perimeter to demonstrate the ease of changing a simple multiple-choice question into another type of assessment.

Unit Tests and Quizzes

Most textbook publishers provide a number of supplemental materials to accompany mathematics textbooks, one of these being a collection of quizzes and unit tests that are aligned with the chapters of the book. Their usefulness varies, and you should take time to review them carefully to determine whether they assess what you wish to assess in the manner you wish to assess it. Tests involving many multiple-choice and short-answer items are easy to administer and to grade, but you need to consider what information you are gathering about the knowledge your students have been developing over the course of the unit. Assessments that are based on recall of facts and procedures are different than those based on students' ability to solve problems and knowledge of when to use relevant facts and procedures. You will want to strike a balance. We start with a typical multiple-choice question on a fifth grade exam:

Find the area and the perimeter of a figure that is 4 feet by 6 feet.

a. A = 20 square feet, P = 24 feet   c. A = 24 square feet, P = 24 feet

b. A = 24 square feet, P = 20 feet   d. A = 10 square feet, P = 12 feet

Unit tests and quizzes, whether written by you or obtained along with the textbook, serve a purpose in assessing students' knowledge. However, to gain a more complete picture of what your students understand, consider other forms of assessment, such as those that follow below.

Open-Middled and Open-Ended Questions

Open-middled questions are questions that students will be able to solve correctly in more than one way. True open-ended questions are questions with more than one correct answer. Open-middled questions are more common in elementary school than open-ended questions. These types of questions require students to show their work, so that teachers can gain insight into their thinking. They allow the teacher to determine the strategies used by the students as well as the manner in which they have carried out their chosen strategy. Here is a modification of the multiple-choice question to an open-middled one:

This is a picture of Farmer Cyrus's garden that is 4 yards by 6 yards. Inside his garden, he has two rectangular areas that cannot be planted. Find the perimeter and the area of land he can plant on.

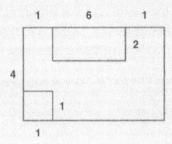

Students can solve this problem by dividing the usable land up into rectangles in a manner similar to the one shown and then adding up the areas (see the following example). Or they could find the area of unusable land and subtract it from the total area of 24 square yards.

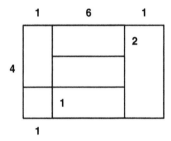

Here are examples of possible open-ended assessments:

1. Create several *different* rectangular gardens with areas that are equivalent to Farmer Cyrus's original garden. Find the perimeter for each of the gardens that you have created.

2. Create several *different* drawings of rectangular gardens that have a perimeter equivalent to Farmer Cyrus's original garden. Find the area for each of the gardens that you have created.

Projects

The benefit for assigning a project is that it enables you to assess higher-level abilities. Problem-solving abilities in particular are difficult to assess in a 40-minute testing situation. Many really interesting problems cannot be solved in 5 minutes and require students to work on them over a period of several days or even weeks. Remember the classic book report that is assigned several weeks in advance, or the solar system project that students often complete in elementary school? Projects in mathematics should be thought of in the same light, as something that requires time to develop and to be completed over a period of time. The following might be used as a mini project when studying area and perimeter.

> Measure the garden behind your school. If your school does not have a garden, find a suitable rectangular piece of land that contains objects such as a fountain, bench, or shed. Find the area and perimeter (or circumference) of each object in the garden and determine the area of usable land for planting vegetables.
>
> To make the garden look nice, you plan to plant some flowers around the perimeter of each object. If you plant flowers 6 inches apart and you would like three rows of flowers around each object, determine how many flowers you will need to plant around the objects.
>
> Create a scale drawing of the garden using a scale of your choice (e.g., 1 inch = 10 feet).

Portfolios

A portfolio is a collection of work that students have completed over a period of time. This can include everything a student has done for an entire unit, including homework, tests, quizzes, and projects, or it may be a specific subset of those items. You may want to ask your students to include several pieces of work in his or her portfolio: the piece of work they are most proud of, what they enjoyed doing the most, the one that needed the most revision, or one worked on further than necessary (a type of extension). The goal for the students in creating a portfolio with specific items of their choosing is to be reflective about the work they have done. They should be encouraged to look at each piece of work with a critical eye and to reflect on the unit as a whole.

Journals

Another means of assessing student progress is through the use of journals. You may also want to use the journal as a means of gauging the affective climate of your classroom related to mathematics. Journals will tell you whether the frustration or satisfaction level is high on any given unit. By assigning prompts such as, "My favorite or least favorite part of this assignment was . . ." you will be able to quickly tell what emotions your students are experiencing as they learn the mathematics.

You may also choose to use the journal as a way to dig deeper into the topic of the day or week. Thinking questions, such as, "Explain why you used multiplication to solve this problem," or "Write down any patterns you noticed in this activity," will encourage students to think more deeply about the concepts presented to them. A journal item involving area and perimeter might look like this:

> Investigate the following statement: As the perimeter of a rectangle increases, the area of a rectangle also increases. Explain your answer using pictures and complete sentences.

Observation and Questioning

Classroom teachers are continually observing, interacting, and collecting information about their students. This information can be used for one or more of the four main purposes of assessment mentioned in the beginning of this chapter: (1) monitoring student progress, (2) making instructional decisions, (3) evaluating student achievement, and (4) evaluating programs. The use of observation and questioning can serve to help you decide what to do next in your instruction as well as inform your pacing and provide evidence for evaluation. Although observation and questioning are generally used by teachers informally, here are some suggestions on ways to formalize what you do naturally as you teach.

Simply documenting your observations and interactions will transform your class time into usable information for assessment. The documentation method you choose will depend on your purposes of assessment. Informal assessment for the purpose of monitoring student progress and making instructional decisions can be documented in a notebook in free form as the observations occur.

An observational checklist to be filled out daily can be as detailed or as minimal as necessary for the students involved. For example, the teacher may keep detailed notes about how much time a student has been on task during the class period or merely use a checklist as simple as this one:

> Name: _____
>
> Date: _____
>
> _____ did/did not participate fully in class today
>
> _____ did/did not complete class work
>
> Notes:

Other instruments, such as the following one that uses a 4-point scale, can be used to evaluate student progress in cooperative learning activities:

Name: _____

1. The student contributed appropriately to the group project. 1 2 3 4

2. The student worked collaboratively. 1 2 3 4

3. Concepts and skills the student learned in this project:

4. Concepts and skills the student still does not understand:

NOTE: 1 is the lowest; 4 is the highest

This tool may be used to determine whether the goals of instruction were met and whether the students are ready to progress to the next topic.

More formal assessments—such as evaluating student performance on a particular problem or set of problems—may take the form of a specific set of questions related to the mathematics in the given problem. For example, if you are assigning grades to the open-ended questions on area and perimeter described in a previous section and you want to ask students questions about their work as part of their grade, you will probably include specific questions, such as these:

1. Describe your method for finding the different rectangular gardens.

2. If you are using whole numbers, how do you know that you have found all the different rectangular gardens of the given area?

3. What patterns did you notice during the solution process?

Observations and questioning can be invaluable tools in both formal and informal assessments used to make on-the-spot changes in a lesson plan or for the next day and coming weeks. As we discussed, this does not need to be a time-intensive or paper-intensive process. Careful preplanning to organize the exact information desired will make the process easier. For further ideas on assessment, see *Mathematics Assessment: A Practical Handbook for Grades 3–5* (NCTM, 2001).

RUBRICS

Rubrics are tools to assess problems that require students to explain their thinking and show their work. Rubrics allow the teacher to look at the final product in a holistic manner focusing on the overall correctness of the solution. Examples follow of holistic rubrics for kindergarten, second, and fourth grade students (Figures 5.1, 5.2, and 5.3).

Figure 5.1 A sample rubric for a kindergarten mathematics assignment

Kindergarten Rubric

 I got the right answer. I understand.

 I made a mistake, but I understand.

 This is too hard!!!!

Figure 5.2 A sample rubric for a second grade mathematics assignment

Second Grade Rubric

3 The student demonstrates understanding of the concept or methods and processes.

2 The student demonstrates some understanding of the concept or methods and processes.

1 The student does not yet demonstrate an understanding of the concept or methods and process.

Figure 5.3   A sample rubric for a fourth grade mathematics assignment

Fourth Grade Rubric

4 The student shows a complete understanding of the problem.
The drawing and words show how the student solved the problem.
The student can explain his or her work using strategies that are grade
appropriate.

3 The student shows an understanding of most of the problem.
The drawing, words, or both that show how the student arrived at the
answer; the answer may contain a few mistakes.
The student can explain his or her answer but may skip some important
details or show little understanding of strategies.

2 The student shows some understanding of the problem.
The drawing, words, or both do not show important details of the problem.
The answer shows several mistakes.

1 The student shows very little understanding of the problem.
The drawing or words cannot be explained by the student.
The answer is wrong.

0 No response

Here is an example of a journal item that could be used in assessing understanding of equivalent fractions in Mr. Callahan's fourth grade classroom (Chapter 1), with sample student responses.

Explain why ¹/₃ = ²/₆. Use pictures and words in your explanation.

We have assessed the student responses using the fourth grade rubric. Here are two examples of student responses with their rating:

Level 2: "I know that to get 2 in the numerator I need to multiply 1 by 2. Because I multiply the numerator and denominator by the same number, the new denominator will be 6. So ¹/₃ = ²/₆. (No pictures are given.)

Level 4: "If I use 1 yellow hexagon for one whole, then ¹/₃ is 1 blue rhombus.

$$= \frac{1}{3}$$

If I need to trade this rhombus for sixths, then I would use the green triangles. The green triangle is half the size of the blue rhombus, so I need twice as many pieces. So I need 2 green triangles, and that will give me ²/₆. So ¹/₃ = ²/₆."

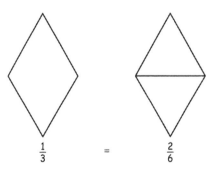

$$\frac{1}{3} \qquad = \qquad \frac{2}{6}$$

The first response was a Level 2 because the response was primarily procedural. The student demonstrated an understanding of *how* to create equivalent fractions but not *why*. No pictures were given. The second response is a Level 4 because the student gave a complete description, using pictures to explain the reasoning.

GRADING AND ASSESSMENT SCHEMES

As you continue to develop your philosophy on assessment, your grading schemes may evolve from one year to the next. In the beginning, many mathematics teachers are inclined to use more traditional testing as a means to assess their learners. However, as time goes by and they obtain more experience with the curriculum, they often begin to see a variety of ways in which student knowledge may be assessed.

One thing we would like for you to consider in developing your grading scheme is the many ways that understanding can be demonstrated. For example, your special needs students or English language learners may perform better in nontraditional assessment tasks, such as projects and other open-ended assignments. This is not to say you should eliminate a formal end-of-chapter exam, but you might want to consider other means of obtaining the same information using a variety of modalities. Some teachers base their entire end-of-quarter or semester grade on just chapter exams and quizzes. Others include individual and group projects, class presentations, and homework, in addition to tests and quizzes. Providing alternative opportunities to express knowledge will better inform you of you students' understanding and abilities.

PRACTICAL WAYS OF ASSESSING THROUGHOUT THE INSTRUCTIONAL PROCESS

Let us reiterate this important point: Assessment can take many forms and should not be limited to formal quizzes, tests, or projects. Remember, assessment is important to inform instruction, and there are multiple opportunities for assessment throughout the instructional process. For example, an informal assessment may take place as you are providing a warm-up problem at the beginning of the class. As the students work on the problem, walk around and observe how the students are progressing, the strategies they are using, and any difficulties they may be encountering. These informal observations may be recorded in a variety of ways. You can mentally take note of the observations, keep written notes in free form, or use a formal checklist to record your findings. Any assigned work can also be used as formal or informal assessment. You can also assess your students through questioning techniques, preplanned activities, and any time used to wrap up the day's activities.

Of course, formal assessments may also be used, such as tests, projects, and quizzes. You might not use each of these types of assessments every day or even every week. However, over the course of an entire unit, you can include quite a few of the different types. You may even want to look at varying your assessments over the course of an entire grading period or even over an entire year. For example, you may include one project per grading period, one journal entry per week, a summative evaluation at the end of the year, and so forth. As you become more comfortable with your teaching, you will more easily focus on what the students are saying and doing in order to craft your instruction.

Instructional Opportunities for Assessment

Warm-Up: You may use the information gathered from warm-ups to further guide your instruction for the remainder of class.

Checking Assigned Work: This may be used either as an informal or formal assessment.

Questioning During Guided Instruction and Activities: This informal means of assessment may provide you with information that can further guide the questions you ask or the activities, examples, and instruction you provide.

Individual Use of Whiteboards: These may be used to encourage individuals to try problems you are presenting without relying on others in the group to do the work. When students are done, ask them to hold up their answers so that you can see how many of them understood the problem.

Group Work: You may request that one paper be turned in that is representative of all the students' thoughts, or randomly collect one student's paper, or request that one student report on his or her findings, either before the end of the class or the next day.

Individual Class Work: This may be checked quickly as you go around the classroom or it may be collected at the end of the class.

Daily Wrap-Up: Depending on the grade level, ask students to either write down what they have learned in class for the day or state it verbally.

Tests and Quizzes: Both of these formal assessments may be given frequently to determine a students' understanding of a concept or skill.

Projects: These may be completed as individual endeavors or as group projects and can generally be used as a means for students to synthesize and apply new concepts. Rubrics are often used to assess student projects.

Portfolios: These assignments require the student to be reflective about the work they have done and can be used to assess student progress over an entire unit of study.

Journals: Journals can be used to encourage deeper thinking about the topic of the day or week as well as to determine student attitudes toward mathematics.

Summative Evaluations: These may be given at the end of the semester or year, depending on the teacher's instructional needs.

TAILORING ASSESSMENTS FOR SPECIAL POPULATIONS

To appropriately assess your special learners, it is essential to consider their individual needs. Does the student have motor difficulties so that writing is larger than normal or is laborious? Does the student have visual processing difficulties that cause him or her to sometimes combine one problem's information and the next? Or is the student an English language learner? All of these needs should be considered, as well as the goals for the assessment, before you create or adapt an existing assessment for a student. All of the assessments we have discussed in this chapter may be modified according to your student's needs in order to obtain information about their mathematical understandings.

Figure 5.4 is an example of an exam prior to modifications made for students with disabilities; Figure 5.5 provides a look at an edited portion of this exam. It demonstrates one possible way to make a test easier to read. Four of the problems are redone; each has extra space for the problem and is boxed off to alleviate confusion. There are reminders for each problem to show work, draw a picture, and write the answer in a complete sentence. The directions are written very clearly, and there are fewer problems per page. In addition, the information needed for Problems 6 and 7 are written out for each one. It may be necessary to include one or two problems per page, depending on the student. All of these modifications create fewer distractions for the student, hopefully allowing for more success.

DATA-DRIVEN INSTRUCTIONAL PRACTICES

Recently, data analysis and the meetings involved with it have become an integral part of many teachers' weekly schedules. Previously, data analysis was primarily left to administrators who traditionally collected the data from state- or district-given tests and provided the analysis for the teachers after the school year has ended. This process has shifted in many schools so that the information gathered may be used to impact instruction immediately. This shift has also included using various forms of assessment, not just high-stakes testing assessments. The goal is to increase student achievement by tailoring instruction on the basis of data collected. Meetings to discuss data can take on a variety of forms depending on the faculty makeup, data collection techniques, and methods of analysis. Typically, teachers meet to discuss a specific grade level and content. For example, sixth grade teachers at one school may decide to create a common assessment tool to assess student understanding of proportional reasoning. They may meet the following week with their students' test

Figure 5.4   Exam prior to modifications made for special needs students

Name: _____

Period: _____

Date: _____

Directions: Solve each problem. Show all of your work, draw a picture to represent your answer, and write your final answer in a complete sentence.

1. Sam picked 33 apples a day for 4 days in a row. How many apples did Sam pick altogether?

2. Joe made $15 a day for 3 days. How much money did Joe have at the end of the third day?

3. There were 32 bees in the flower garden. Farmer Jenny could catch 8 bees at a time in her net. How many times did she have to use her net to catch the bees?

4. Daniel caught 12 butterflies each day for 6 days. On the seventh day, 2 butterflies escaped. How many butterflies did he have left?

(Continued)

(Continued)

5. Arifa had 16 friends she wanted to invite to her house for lunch. If each friend eats 1 hamburger and drinks 2 glasses of soda, how many hamburgers and how many sodas does she have to buy?

Use the following information for Problems 6 and 7.

Amy and Evonne are roommates who share an apartment. They have three payments they must make each month: Rent for the apartment is $300, electricity is $20, and their phone charges are $40. They each individually pay for their own food.

6. What do Amy and Evonne each pay per month to live in their apartment?

7. If a third roommate, Trisha, moves in the apartment, how much would each roommate then pay to live in the apartment?

From Sliva, J.A. (2003). *Teaching Inclusive Mathematics to Special Learners, K–6*. Thousand Oaks, CA: Corwin Press, www.corwinpress.com.

Figure 5.5 Exam with modifications made for special needs students

Name: _____

Period: _____

Date: _____

Directions: Solve each equation.

- Show all of your work.
- Draw a picture to represent your answer.
- Write your final answer in a complete sentence.

1. Sam picked 33 apples a day for 4 days in a row. How many apples did Sam pick altogether?

   Draw a picture: Work:

   Answer in a complete sentence:

2. Joe made $15 a day for 3 days. How much money did Joe have at the end of the third day?

   Draw a picture: Work:

   Answer in a complete sentence:

(Continued)

(Continued)

6. Amy and Evonne are roommates and share an apartment. They have three payments they must make each month: Rent for the apartment is $300, electricity is $20, and their phone charges are $40. They each individually pay for their own food.

   What do Amy and Evonne each pay per month to live in their apartment?

   Draw a picture: Work:

   Answer in a complete sentence:

7. Amy and Evonne are roommates and share an apartment. They have three monthly payments they must make: rent for the apartment is $300, electricity is $20, and their phone charges are $40. They each individually pay for their own food.

   If a third roommate, Trisha, moves into the apartment, how much would each roommate then pay to live in the apartment?

   Draw a picture: Work:

   Answer in a complete sentence:

From Sliva, J.A. (2003). *Teaching Inclusive Mathematics to Special Learners, K–6*. Thousand Oaks, CA: Corwin Press, www.corwinpress.com.

scores to discuss the results. The discussion of these results is generally aimed at answering questions such as these:

1. Did the students master the material taught?

2. Were there any specific concepts or skills that the students did not master?

3. What were the instructional strategies used to instruct those skills or concepts? Were they appropriate?

4. If any remediation is needed, how and when will it be provided?

5. What are the next steps for instruction?

The questions addressed at such a meeting may vary, depending on the needs of the faculty. Generally, the goals are to inspect the data, determine remediation steps if necessary, and then plan for the next instructional steps. These meetings may be mandated at many schools or may be set up informally by groups of teachers to help them better tailor instruction to meet their students' needs.

A WORD ABOUT STANDARDIZED TESTS

Assessments fall under two major categories: criterion-referenced and norm-referenced. In most schools, classroom assessments that are administered by the classroom teacher are criterion-referenced assessments. According to FairTest: The National Center for Fair and Open Testing (n.d.), "Criterion-referenced tests are intended to measure how well a person has learned a specific body of knowledge and skills" (¶ 1). This is in contrast to norm-referenced tests. Many of the norm-referenced major exams that students take are commonly called *standardized* tests. Two examples are the Scholastic Aptitude Test (SAT) and the California Achievement Test (CAT). A student's score depends on the performance of others who have taken the same assessment. Scores are placed along the normal distribution (bell-shaped curve) and then students are given a score relative to others' standings. In short, in a criterion-referenced assessment, students are judged relative to a predetermined performance standard or criterion. In a norm-referenced assessment, students are judged relative to the performance of other students taking the test.

SUMMARY

Backward-design assessment is a complex process that requires you to have clear goals for your students, tailor instruction to meet these goals using knowledge about the students, and then use an appropriate method to assess the students' mathematical understandings. The use of the backward design method discussed in this chapter will help you to gear your instruction to the desired outcomes, rather than trying to find an appropriate assessment instrument after the fact. The discussion of different types of assessments should guide you in adapting commercially made assessments to meet your different evaluation needs. This component of instruction is more important than ever because assessment is being used more widely to make team-based and school-based decisions on what to teach and what to reteach.

6 Putting It All Together

Now that you have read about many of the important elements that make up a successful mathematics class, it's time to think about how it all fits together. In this chapter, we discuss ways for you to incorporate the core themes of this book throughout your mathematics curriculum. We show you how to connect big ideas within mathematics, and we present ideas for you to connect mathematics with other subjects.

THE YEAR AT A GLANCE: DESIGNING YOUR CURRICULUM

One of the most crucial components of teaching is being well versed in your content area. Your education has provided experiences for you to grow in your understanding of the mathematics content you will be teaching in elementary school. When creating your curriculum, you will use that content knowledge, in addition to making decisions about what topics will be presented, how you will present the topics, and how long you will spend on each one. This task is often referred to as a *scope and sequence*. Well before you begin your first day of class, you will spend countless hours behind the scenes determining each element of your scope and sequence.

One important distinction to be aware of is that a mathematics text is not a curriculum; it is just a text. A curriculum is much more. Although each teacher at your grade level in your school will be using the same book, the way you choose to implement the ideas in the text may be very different. It is the group of mathematical experiences, together with materials, that make up a curriculum.

To begin, you should have a framework from which to pull your curriculum. As we discussed in Chapter 2, there are standards documents that explicitly describe the content that students should learn at each grade level. These documents, along with any school or district standards, are an excellent foundation from which to begin the development of your curriculum. Next, materials should be gathered that may be used to teach mathematics throughout the year. When developing a scope and sequence, it is most helpful if you can work with another individual who is experienced at teaching the specific content or age group, or if you have a previously developed scope and sequence on which to model your own.

A syllabus for your course may also need to be created. A syllabus forms part of the overall curriculum and usually includes the standards to be addressed, a suggested time line of instruction, and a grading scheme. Although in many elementary schools a syllabus is not normally passed out to students, it is helpful to have this information for your planning purposes. Again, other teachers in your school who have taught this content and age group may have a syllabus that you can use as a guide to create your own. Once the curriculum has been selected, begin to think about your grading scheme. Assessment requirements can vary from school to school. First check to see if your school has a grading system or scheme that you are required to use. If there is no set grading system, ask a colleague who has taught the same grade level if you could use or adapt his or her system. Your thoughts and philosophy about assessment may change over time and so may your assessment scheme. However, it is often difficult to change a scheme during an academic year. If significant changes are to be made, consider revising for the following year.

Once you have developed your scope and sequence, this does not mean that you are not allowed to deviate from the plan. Each year your students will arrive with different needs and abilities, based on their different mathematics backgrounds. For example, you may find you need to review multiples and how to determine common denominators when you thought you were not going to need to; this could change your time line and alter your curriculum. As time progresses, you will gain a greater understanding of the students you are teaching at your age range as well as the content to be taught.

MAKING CONNECTIONS WITHIN MATHEMATICS

It may seem like a lot to ask teachers to cover all of the mandated standards as well as each section in the book. Indeed, many new (and not so new) teachers become overwhelmed trying to teach everything in the curriculum for their grade level. It may help to look at mathematics more holistically, instead of focusing on each lesson as a separate entity. If you view mathematics as a connected body of knowledge instead of a disjointed set of rules and ideas, it will be easier to adequately cover all of the standards. One approach is to incorporate activities into your instruction that address more than one concept at a time. For example, the four operations of arithmetic are connected in many ways. Recall the second grade vignette from Chapter 1 in which Miss Barilla makes the connections between addition and subtraction. A lesson using real-world problems whose solutions involve two or more of these operations can be a great way for students to gain more experience with the concepts and skills underlying these operations. Although you may not actually teach all of the operations at once, you can spend less time on them initially knowing that you will integrate these ideas in future lessons. A third grade teacher introducing multiplication can also introduce the concept of division through use of real-world examples involving sharing. Often the same scenarios used to study multiplication can be adapted to present the concept of division. The multiplication scenario could be similar to the following: There are 5 children and they each bring 3 cookies to class. How many cookies are there altogether? When adapted for division, it could look like this: There are 15 cookies, and you want to share them equally among 5 children. How many cookies does each child receive?

Let us also consider the following two-part activity:

The Perfect Party Place

Dan Sullivan has his own business, the Perfect Party Place. He entertains children on their birthdays. After providing some entertainment, Dan sets up card tables for children to have cake and ice cream. All the tables are square, and only one child can sit on each side of a table (Phillips, 1991; Roddick & Bergthold, 2004).

Part A. Mr. Sullivan has a party booked this Saturday for 18 children, and he wants to place the tables in a rectangle. How many different ways can he seat the 18 children?

Part B. Mr. Sullivan has another party booked for the following Saturday, and the customer, Mr. Jones, has told him the space available for the tables is 24 square units. How many different ways can he set up the card tables in a rectangular formation so that the children can sit together? What is the minimum number of children that can be invited? What is the maximum number of children that can be invited?

This problem is an example of how several concepts in mathematics can be addressed at one time. For example, in the first scenario the perimeter is fixed, and students are asked to investigate different areas that correspond to the perimeter of 18. Students must use their knowledge of area and perimeter as well as their understanding of the definition of a rectangle. The way this question is worded, the table arrangement must be a rectangle.

For example, if a student draws a picture or uses tiles, here is one possible solution for Part A.

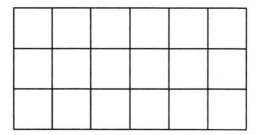

An investigation of the area of nonregular shapes could also be included in this activity if the shape of the tables was altered to include empty space in the middle or make an L-shaped configuration, for example.

In Part B the area is fixed, and students investigate the change in perimeter. This activity ties nicely into a study of factors and gives tangible evidence of how factors are used. Students discover the connection between the dimensions of the different tables and the factors of 24. One possible arrangement a student may arrive at is as follows:

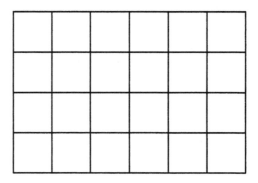

This activity is rich in that it speaks to more than one mathematical concept and, even more, demonstrates the connectedness of mathematical ideas. Whether you are introducing factors and reinforcing ideas of area and perimeter or vice versa, this activity will allow you to address more than one item on your seemingly endless list of curricular requirements. When developing your curriculum, search for activities such as this one, which address more than one concept at once. This should be one of your criteria when deciding whether or not to include a particular activity in your lessons.

Note: This activity may be enriched by connecting it to the book *Spaghetti and Meatballs for All* by Marilyn Burns (1997).

MAKING CONNECTIONS ACROSS THE CURRICULUM

Another way to approach the task of teaching all of the standards is to integrate mathematics into other content areas whenever possible. Not only does integrating mathematics in other content areas reinforce the use of the mathematics, but it also allows you more time to teach mathematics, and as a result more mathematics can be covered throughout the year. Self-contained classrooms provide an excellent opportunity to make connections between and among different subjects.

Mathematics in Language Arts

Increased literacy is a high priority throughout the country; schools are consistently working toward raising their students' achievement in both reading and writing. Recall from the discussion about communication in the mathematics classroom in Chapter 2 that a student's ability to explain how they arrived at a solution both verbally and in writing is a goal of the National Council of Teachers of Mathematics. Thus, by increasing communication (both in writing and verbally) in your mathematics classroom, you are working to increase a student's literacy in both language arts and mathematics. Writing may be implemented in your mathematics class in a variety of ways. It could be as simple as asking your students to explain their answers in full sentences or as involved as assigning a project in which students have to write up the solution to a problem, including their findings and conclusions in a report. You may decide that you want to have a weekly journal entry in which students write about their successes and frustrations learning mathematics. Whatever approach you take, you will want to make sure to expect high-quality writing as well as high-quality mathematics.

Another aspect of literacy is reading. There are a number of excellent books that involve mathematical concepts in their story line. Students enjoy listening to their teachers read stories, and the use of mathematics within literature can be a tool to engage your class in the topic of the day. Students may read stories to increase their depth of comprehension as well as their knowledge of mathematics. There is a great deal of literature that contains connections to mathematics at a variety of content and age-appropriate levels. In addition to reading these books, having students read mathematics textbooks and word problems also helps to reinforce important reading skills within a content area, skills that students need in order to be successful throughout their education. (See Appendix B for a list of children's books focusing on mathematics.)

Amanda Bean's Amazing Dream (Neuschwander, 1998) is one such book. This story is used by Ms. Heinz in the following vignette to introduce the concept of multiplication at the end of the second grade.

Vignette 1: Second Grade—Multiplication

It is near the end of the school year, and Ms. Heinz wants to introduce multiplication to her students. She begins her lesson on multiplication by reading Amanda Bean's Amazing Dream *to her students (Neuschwander, 1998). As she reads, she tells the story of Amanda, a girl about their age, who loves to count everything. "I am Amanda Bean and I count anything and everything!" Ms. Heinz reads (p. 16). Amanda's teacher has told her she should learn the multiplication facts, but Amanda confidently tells him that she can get the same answer just by counting.*

Throughout the story, Amanda encounters many items in rows and columns and becomes more and more frustrated by her inefficient method of determining how many there are. Finally, in a dream in which she goes crazy trying to count every-thing at once, she understands the importance of multiplying. Upon waking, she immediately tells her mother that today will be the day she begins to learn the mul-tiplication facts.

After Ms. Heinz finishes the story, she talks to her class about multiplication. She points out the cookies in the bakery found in the book, all lined up in 6 rows and 3 columns, and she asks her students how they can find out how many cook-ies there are in all. Some of them respond by counting all of them, just like Amanda Bean has done in the book. Others notice that you can add 6+6+6 or 3+3+3+3+3+3 to get the answer. Ms. Heinz uses this discussion to make the con-nection between repeated addition and multiplication and reiterates the lesson learned by Amanda that multiplication is a quicker way to get the answer than counting or repeatedly adding.

As Ms. Heinz passes out one-inch-square tiles and the class activity for the day, students join their preassigned groups. The problems are as follows:

1. Ms. Napier, the lunch lady, has 5 rows of pizza on the pan. Each row has 2 pieces of pizza in it. Using your blocks, show how many pieces of pizza she has in her pan. Then, on your worksheet, draw how many pieces of pizza she has and write down the total number. Explain how you found your answer.

2. In a van, there are 4 rows of seats from front to back, and 3 people can sit in each row. How many people can fit in the van? Show your answer using the blocks. Draw your answer on the worksheet and state how many students are in the van. Explain how you got your answer. Can you think of another way to explain your answer?

The students have never worked with multiplication prior to this, so Ms. Heinz is focused on them working with the concrete representation first, moving to pictorial representations, and then determining the answers in symbolic form. However, she is not requiring the students to memorize their multiplication tables; she is concerned with the students gaining a conceptual understanding of multiplication because she knows this is the foundation from which many of their future understandings of mathematics will occur. As she walks around the room, she makes mental notes and handwritten ones about which students are participating in their pairs; as she does so, she asks students questions and encourages those who are not participating fully. After she is convinced all students have tried the three problems and discussed them within their groups, she asks a pair of students to present their answer. She then asks if anyone can think of a different way to solve the problems.

For homework, students are asked to look around their classroom and their home and to come up with a problem that can be solved using multiplication. The next day, students will continue working on their concrete representations of multiplication and discuss the problems they created. During this unit, students will progress through the three phases of representation: using concrete objects, drawing pictures, and using symbols (numbers) to solve multiplication problems. By the end of the unit, students will have the opportunity to write their own stories about multiplication. These stories will be displayed in the hallways of the school and within the classroom.

Note that Ms. Heinz has captured her students' attention by beginning the mathematics lesson with a story. Second graders delight in having their teacher read to them, and this book is used to lay the foundation for all of the elements important for an introductory lesson on multiplication. By using this story, Ms. Heinz is able to incorporate literature and mathematics into a single lesson as well as engage her students both cognitively, behaviorally, and affectively.

Mathematics Within Science

One of the goals of mathematics instruction is that students understand mathematics and be able to apply that knowledge to other courses. Science is a subject that focuses on inquiry and makes frequent use of mathematics. Inquiry is a process that is heavily dependent upon the area of statistics, including skills such as hypothesis, data collection, and analysis. The inquiry process relies on good computational, problem-solving, and reasoning skills. In addition, mathematics may be integrated into a variety of science topics, such as weather. Connections between probability and the likelihood of rain over a span of days may be made by having students investigate the meaning of the statement, "There is an 80% chance of rain tomorrow."

When studying the history of flight, you may include a project in which students use their knowledge of plane aerodynamics to build their own planes. Students can participate in a class contest to determine which planes fly the farthest or the longest. Hang time (the amount of time a plane is in air) and distance flown can be collected for each plane and subsequently analyzed. If your students are currently studying statistics, you can ask them to determine the mean, median, and mode of the hang time and distance. If your class is studying percentages or fractions, you can ask questions such as, "What percent of the planes flew more than 20 feet?"

Dinosaurs are another popular topic studied in elementary science. Students may be asked to estimate the amount of food a specific type of dinosaur ate over time using their computational and problem-solving skills. Using their knowledge of ratio and proportion, they can be asked to create a reduced-scale drawing of a dinosaur.

Some resources for developing curricula that tie mathematics and science together may be found at the following Web sites:

- AIMS Educational Foundation. www.aimsedu.org/
- The Lawrence Hall of Science. www.lawrencehallofscience.org/
- The Institute for Mathematics and Science Education. www.math .uic.edu/~imse/IMSE/
- The Teaching Integrated Mathematics and Science (TIMS) Project. www.math.uic.edu/~imse/IMSE/TIMS/tims.html

Mathematics Within Art

Mathematics and art are closely connected; the content area of geometry is a natural connection that is often made with art. Famous artists, such as da Vinci or M. C. Escher, were well aware of mathematical patterns that occur in nature, and they reproduced those visually appealing patterns in their paintings. Two of the mathematical connections da Vinci used in addition to patterning are the Fibonacci sequence and the golden ratio. The golden ratio (approximately 1.616) occurs repeatedly in the measurements of the human body. For example, the ratio of the length of the arm to the length from the elbow to the end of the hand is approximately the golden ratio.

The study of tessellations provides another engaging example of mathematics and art. Students can investigate which of the regular polygons tessellate a plane (tile it without any gaps or overlaps) and make the connection to the measurement of the interior angles. An in-depth example of an activity involving tessellations is given in Chapter 4.

Fractals are also a popular topic involving mathematics and art that is accessible to elementary students. Sierpinski's Triangle and the Koch Snowflake are two well-known fractals that provide interesting investigations in area, perimeter, fractions, and algebraic generalization of patterns.

Some resources for mathematics and art connections follow:

- Golden Ratios. http://math.rice.edu/~lanius/Geom/golden.html
- Tessellations. www.tessellations.org/
- Tessellation Tutorials. http://mathforum.org/sum95/suzanne/tess.intro.html
- Ranucci, E. R., & Teeters, J. L. (1977). *Creating Escher-type drawings.* Mountain View, CA: Creative Publications.
- A Fractals Unit for Elementary and Middle School Students. http://math.rice.edu/~lanius/frac/

Mathematics Within the Social Sciences

The study of populations in social studies lends itself nicely to the inclusion of mathematics. As with science, statistics and its related understandings are easily integrated into the content. Students can create bar graphs of different populations over time and note any sharp increases or decreases. These changes can be linked to events of historical significance, such as war, disease, and so forth. Presidential elections, apportionment of congressional seats, and voting can be used as an opportunity to make use of mathematics. By knowing the number of electoral votes each state has and how many are needed to win the presidency, students can create various scenarios for different ways each candidate could possibly win the election. The use of results from election polling and the knowledge of states that historically support a particular party, as well as the key swing states, can be incorporated to make this a rich, ongoing activity.

Creating Thematic Lessons

Extending the previous idea, here follows a theme-based lesson that draws from several subjects. During a presidential election year, you can capitalize on current events to discuss the platforms of different candidates running for office. Depending on the grade you are teaching, you may want to bring in only one or two main differences in platforms among the candidates or you may want to ask your students to find several differences in the candidates' positions on important issues. Geography can be studied as you track the candidates' speeches around the United States. States can be identified as "blue" or "red" depending on the reporting of the polls.

Students can learn about the statistics involved in the election polling and projection process. They can then conduct their own poll in their school or town to determine public opinion on popular issues or candidates. Students can also use mathematics to determine the various combinations of states necessary to win the election. There will be more than one possible scenario depending on how close the race is projected to be, and students should be asked to come up with more than one possible answer.

Language arts could be incorporated into this project by reading a book about presidents or elections to introduce the theme. *Duck for President* (Cronin, 2004) will appeal to the younger elementary grades; older students could read a short biography of a president. Students could also be asked to write a position paper, giving reasons they would support a particular candidate or defending their possible scenarios for winning the electoral votes of particular states.

We have only scratched the surface of all the ways in which you can infuse mathematics throughout your curriculum. Keep your eye out for others as you continue to create your lesson plans for the year. In addition, if you are working within a school that provides planning time within grade levels, this can present an excellent opportunity to share ideas and create activities that integrate multiple content areas and focus on current events and schoolwide themes.

MATHEMATICAL CONNECTIONS ACROSS GRADES

Within your self-contained classroom, you have many opportunities to connect mathematics to other disciplines, as we have discussed. These opportunities are within your reach and can become a strong part of your multisubject curriculum as you entwine all your subjects together into a strong, cohesive body of knowledge. That being said, it is also wise to consider what other teachers are doing with your students both before you receive them and after you have taught them for a year. Mathematics is often taught in a spiraling manner, revisiting topics each year and building on previous knowledge to further understanding of each concept. Although schools often provide planning time within grade levels, it is not as common to find teachers discussing the teaching and learning of mathematics across several grade levels to determine what the focus should be each year. For this reason, it is not unheard of for certain topics to become lost. This can occur when one teacher assumes the topic will be taught in the following year, whereas the teacher of the higher grade believes that the topic has already been taught before the students reach his or her class. Both touching base informally in an ongoing manner and connecting formally to determine the depth of knowledge reached at each grade level will go a long way toward ensuring that students receive the appropriate amount and level of instruction.

Another important consideration is the manner in which a certain topic has been taught. Take the fraction example from Chapter 1. Mr. Callahan chose to approach the teaching of fractions in the fourth grade in a hands-on manner using pattern blocks. In the next year, it would benefit the students if the fifth grade teacher could build on this approach. Consider the following scenario:

Vignette 2: Fourth and Fifth Grade Collaboration

Miss Jackson is a fifth grade teacher in the same school where Mr. Callahan teaches fourth grade. The two often discuss their mathematics curricula during lunch, and Mr. Callahan has intrigued Miss Jackson with his hands-on approach to fractions. Last year, Miss Jackson decided to continue the same hands-on approach in the fifth grade, extending the understanding to real-world problems involving addition, subtraction, multiplication, and division of fractions. She decided to begin each lesson by introducing a real-world problem that involves arithmetic of fractions. She has students work in groups with pattern blocks to create a hands-on model of the problem, and they are also asked to create their own pictures to model it. The steps they take to solve the problem using the pictures and the blocks are then shared with the rest of the class.

Using division as an example, students could model the following problem, 4 ÷ 2/3, with the pattern blocks:

> *You want to make some pies, and you have 4 cups of flour. Each pie takes 2/3 of a cup of flour. How many pies can you make?*

This problem involves the measurement (repeated subtraction) model of division, so students can solve this problem by repeatedly subtracting 2/3 from 4 until they can no longer subtract 2/3 anymore. (They have experienced the measurement model previously when they learned division with whole numbers, so this problem is just an extension into fractions.) When using pattern blocks, 4 yellow hexagons could be used to represent the 4 cups of flour. Students will then need to determine how many groups of 2/3 are found in 4. One yellow hexagon is equivalent to 3 blue rhombuses, so they can trade each of the yellow hexagons for 3 blue rhombuses, for a total of 12 blue rhombuses. Each of the blue rhombuses represents 1/3 of a cup of flour, so the rhombuses need to be arranged into groups of 2, with each group representing 2/3 of the whole hexagon. Students can then find that the answer is 6 simply by counting the groups of pattern blocks.

Miss Jackson uses their invented techniques as a way to connect their models and solution methods to the actual computations involved in solving the problem procedurally. When discussing the division problem 4 ÷ 2/3, she points out that, by trading each yellow hexagon in for 3 blue rhombuses, you are multiplying 4 by 3. When you arrange the rhombuses into groups of two, you are actually dividing 12 by 2. When you combine these two steps, you can see that the problem was solved by multiplying 4 by 3 and dividing by 2, which is precisely the "invert and multiply" procedure. This method of teaching allows students to more fully participate in the learning process, and it's a richer learning experience than simply memorizing the steps for each computation. Furthermore, students are actively engaged in the process of determining a solution method for each problem, because Miss Jackson has not yet shown them a step-by-step process. This approach will increase their understanding of the real-world problem and encourage them to construct their own knowledge about problems involving fractions.

When teachers at different grade levels collaborate, like Mr. Callahan and Miss Jackson have, students benefit from a more cohesive learning experience. The timing using manipulatives and other teaching methods has been agreed on at these two grade levels, so students do not need to continually adjust to different teaching philosophies. There is sufficient time given at each grade level to develop a strong conceptual understanding of fractions through use of pattern blocks. Once this has been established, procedures can then be introduced.

This chapter has provided you with examples of how to incorporate the ideas in the book into your mathematics lessons. For more information on growing as a professional, see Appendix C.

SUCCEEDING AT TEACHING MATHEMATICS—AND LOVING IT!

In this book, we have provided you with some food for thought on the many intricacies involved in teaching and learning mathematics. Ultimately, you need to be convinced that what you are doing in the classroom is the best for your students' mathematical development. Try out the ideas and principles from this book so that you can begin to determine how you can make them best work for you and become part of your overall teaching philosophy.

As a new teacher of mathematics, you will go a long distance toward professional confidence and significantly impact the way your students perform in your mathematics class if you start the year well. Very often, new teachers concentrate so hard on their instruction and materials that they lose sight of the students. A major message of this book is to keep students front and center. Connect with your students and recognize their needs. Give them clear expectations and a safe, engaging learning environment. It is important for you as a teacher to be aware of the various problems students may experience while learning mathematics. By paying close attention, you can help each student do well.

In the beginning of the first chapter, we painted a scenario of your first day of school. We hope that at this point, you feel more prepared to take on the challenges that teachers of mathematics continually face. Although each day may not be perfect, we hope that you do not lose sight of your goals and your reasons for choosing this profession in the first place. Although this book is focused on ways to engage the student in learning mathematics, do your best to make sure that you are engaged in the teaching process as well. It is a journey that you embark on with your students and, as important as it is for the students to enjoy the journey, it is just as important for you to enjoy what you have worked so hard to create.

Appendix A

Communicating With Families

Although most of your time is spent inside your classroom with students, the parents and guardians of your students are important contacts throughout the year. Although your encounters with parents will often be brief, taking initial steps to forge positive relationships will serve you well over the years. There are several key moments throughout the year when you will want to put your best foot forward with parents: two of those are the first day of school and back-to-school night.

Communicating About Mathematics Teaching and Learning

Clear communication with parents enables the development of positive relationships and makes conversations go much more smoothly. The first day or week of school, send home as much information as possible about the material the class will be learning throughout the year, classroom expectations, and opportunities for communication with you, the teacher. Many parents have concerns about their children's education, especially in the area of mathematics. Providing this information tends to alleviate many fears and opens the door for good communication.

Be prepared for parents and guardians questioning how you are teaching, what you are teaching, and why. This can occur because of shifts in mathematics standards across the country. Other issues may arise with regard to homework, cooperative learning, instructional strategies, calculator usage, and the use of manipulatives. Remember, the NCTM standards for mathematics were developed in 1989 and revised again in 2000. Many parents and guardians base their expectations about their children's classes on their own experiences learning mathematics 20–40 years ago. In that time, a lot has changed. For example, many parents and guardians may never have used a calculator when learning mathematics during their primary school days. They may also have never used manipulatives and are unfamiliar with how they are used to teach mathematics. To communicate effectively with parents, you need to be open to discussions about their concerns and about *your* teaching. Then you may use documents such as the NCTM *Principles and Standards for Teaching Mathematics* and your state and district standards to discuss the importance and necessity for the mathematics you teach and the methods you use. Also turn to your colleagues for assistance and ideas on communicating with parents on these issues.

Back-to-School Night

When you think of back-to-school night, you should think information, information, information. This night is one of the few chances you will have to give parents and guardians information about the kind of year they can expect for their child. This is an excellent time to clarify the many issues and questions that parents and guardians may have about their children's mathematical learning experience (see previous discussion), as it is also one of the few times you will see many of your students' parents. For this reason, you may want to touch base with parents and guardians either by phone or by mail prior to the event to communicate the importance of their attendance. Capitalize on the short time you have to make a connection with each parent. This first interaction can pave the way for productive future correspondence.

Here are some important considerations when planning for back-to-school night:

• Communicate your philosophy of teaching and learning mathematics. Display copies of the textbook and other resources you will be using, such as manipulatives and supplemental books. Invite parents to view these materials after you have explained your approach to teaching mathematics. Copies of your syllabus and daily class schedule should also be available, as well as any specific rules pertaining to your classroom.

• Create a folder for each student and have it readily available for the parents. Include some mathematics work that each student has completed in these first few weeks. If possible, include an interesting activity your students have completed in mathematics recently, one that illustrates the type of learning that will take place throughout the year. Have a mathematics activity ready for your parents to try if there is time. Consider putting a mathematics problem on the board that represents the type of teaching and instruction you will be using throughout the year.

- Last but not least, express enthusiasm for teaching and learning mathematics and for your students. Let parents and guardians know that this is a subject you care about and that you are using up-to-date research and standards to teach their children. And assure them that it will be a great year for their child.

Your main goal for back-to-school night is to communicate with your students' parents and guardians. Let them know who you are and how they can expect you to teach their child mathematics. Convey your love of children as well as your love for teaching. Most important, pave the way for future positive communication with parents and guardians.

Use of Class Web Pages

A Web page is also an excellent tool to communicate with parents. Each week or month, a teacher can place new information or updates on the Web page to communicate with parents. Often teachers use the Web as a means to communicate homework assignments with parents. Some teachers use it to display student work. You may also want to use it to recommend Web sites for students to learn about mathematics.

There are an enormous number of Web sites that contain information for mathematics teachers, from lesson plans to discussion boards. As previously mentioned, the NCTM Web site (www.nctm.org) is an excellent resource for your own professional growth, and it is also great for obtaining resources for teaching your students. Here are a few others:

- Ask Dr. Math. www.mathforum.org./dr.math/
- Virtual Manipulatives. www.arcytech.org/java/patterns/patterns_j.shtml
- PBS Teacher Source. www.pbs.org/teachersource/math.htm
- AIMS Education Foundation. www.aimsedu.org/puzzle/index.html
- Family Math. www.lhs.berkeley.edu/equals/FMnetwork.html

Appendix B

Mathematics and Literature Connections

Anno, M., & Anno, M. (1983). *Mysterious multiplying jar.* New York: Penguin. (Topics: Multiplication and factorials)

Axelrod, A. (1997). *Pigs will be pigs.* New York: Simon & Schuster. (Topic: Money)

Birch, D. (1988). *The king's chessboard.* New York: Penguin. (Topic: Exponential)

Burns, M. (1995). *The greedy triangle.* New York: Scholastic. (Topic: Polygons)

Burns, M. (1997). *Spaghetti and meatballs for all.* New York: Scholastic. (Topics: Perimeter, patterns)

Derubertis, B. (1999). *A collection for Kate* (Math Matters Series). New York: Kane. (Topics: Basic counting and addition strategies such as counting on, using doubles, estimating, and regrouping)

Giganti, P., Jr. (1999). *Each orange had 8 slices.* New York: HarperTrophy. (Topics: Counting, repeated addition, multiplication)

Hutchins, P. (1986). *The doorbell rang.* New York: Greenwillow. (Topic: Division—sharing model)

McGrath, M. M. (1994). *The M&M's counting book.* Watertown, MA: Charlesbridge. (Topic: Counting)

McGrath, M. M. (1998). *More M&M's math.* Watertown, MA: Charlesbridge. (Topics: Addition, division, multiplication, ordinal numbers, and graphing)

Myller, R. (1962). *How big is a foot?* New York: Bantam Doubleday Dell. (Topic: Measurement)

Neuschwander, C. (1997). *Sir Cumference and the first round table.* Watertown, MA: Charlesbridge. (Topics: Geometry, polygons, circles, diameter)

Neuschwander, C. (1998). *Amanda Bean's amazing dream.* New York: Scholastic. (Topics: Counting, adding in groups, multiplication)

Neuschwander, C. (1999). *Sir Cumference and the dragon of Pi.* Watertown, MA: Charlesbridge. (Topic: Circles)

Neuschwander, C. (2001). *Sir Cumference and the great knight of Angleland.* Watertown, MA: Charlesbridge. (Topic: Geometry—circles)

Neuschwander, C. (2003). *Sir Cumference and the sword in the cone.* Watertown, MA: Charlesbridge. (Topic: Geometry—volume)

Pinczes, E. (1995). *A remainder of one.* Boston: Houghton Mifflin. (Topics: Division, remainders, factors)

Pinczes, E. (1999). *One hundred hungry ants.* Boston: Houghton Mifflin. (Topics: Multiplication, division, factors)

Pittman, H. C. (1995). *A grain of rice.* New York: Yearling. (Topics: Doubling, exponential growth, large numbers)

Schwartz, D. (1999). *If you hopped like a frog.* New York: Scholastic. (Topics: Ratio and proportion)

Schwartz, D. M. (1999). *G is for googol: A math alphabet book.* Berkeley, CA: Tricycle Press. (Topics: A variety of mathematical topics)

Schwartz, D. M. (1985). *How much is a million?* New York: HarperCollins. (Topic: Large numbers—million, billion, trillion)

Tang, G. (2001). *The grapes of math.* New York: Scholastic. (Topics: Counting, addition)

Tompert, A. (1990). *Grandfather Tang's story.* New York: Crown. (Topic: Geometry—using tangrams)

Wells, R. E. (1993). *Is a blue whale the biggest thing there is?* Morton Grove, IL: Albert Whitman. (Topics: Measurement, number sense with large numbers)

Appendix C

Growing as a Professional

There are several professional organizations that may help with your professional growth as an elementary teacher. An important information source for your professional development in mathematics is the National Council of Teachers of Mathematics (NCTM), the major professional organization for K–12 teachers of mathematics. This organization consists of individuals who teach mathematics K–12, as well as collegiate mathematics educators and other mathematics specialists. NCTM has many resources helpful to you at your particular grade level: regular issues of mathematics teacher journals, local and national conferences focused on ideas for the mathematics classroom, professional course offerings, as well as written references. Your district may have a membership to NCTM, but you may want to join yourself to receive many of its benefits personally.

At the elementary level, NCTM offers a journal titled *Teaching Children Mathematics*. This journal is published monthly and is available both electronically and as a printed journal. It offers up-to-date information about the state of mathematics education in elementary education as well as activities for your students. There are also several conferences to choose from, both regionally and nationally, each year. These conferences provide a plethora of sessions, most of which are standards-based activities that you can use in your classroom. More information about this organization can be found at www.nctm.org.

In addition to this national professional organization, there are many state and local organizations that are also extremely beneficial to your professional development. A mathematics specialist in your district will be aware of these organizations, or you may contact NCTM for a listing of those organizations in your local area. As with NCTM, these organizations typically have yearly conferences, and some publish their own journals.

References

Baxter, J. A., Woodward, J., & Olson, D. (2001). Effects of reform-based mathematics instruction on low achievers in five third-grade classrooms. *The Elementary School Journal, 101*(5), 529–547.

Bley, N. S, & Thornton, C. A. (2001). *Teaching mathematics to students with learning disabilities* (4th ed.). Austin, TX: PRO-ED.

Bresser, R. (2003). Helping English-language learners develop computational fluency. *Teaching Children Mathematics, 9,* 294–299.

Brown, H. D. (2001). *Teaching by principles: An interactive approach to language pedagogy* (2nd ed.). White Plains, NY: Longman.

Bruner, J. (1966). *Toward a theory of instruction.* Cambridge, MA: Harvard University Press.

Burns, M. (1997). *Spaghetti and meatballs for all.* New York: Scholastic.

Collier, V. P. (1989). How long? A synthesis of research on academic achievement in a second language. *TESOL Quarterly, 23,* 509–531.

Connolly, P. (1989). Writing and the ecology of learning. In P. Connolly & T. Valardi (Eds.), *Writing to learn mathematics and science* (pp. 1–14). New York: Teachers College Press.

Cronin, D. (2004). *Duck for president.* New York: Scholastic Press.

FairTest: The National Center for Fair & Open Testing. (n.d.). *Criterion- and standards-reference tests.* Retrieved April 23, 2007 from http://www.fairtest.org/facts/csrtests.html

Glasser, W. (1992). *The quality school: Managing students without coercion.* New York: Harper Perennial.

Grouws, D. A., & Cebulla, K. J. (2000). *Improving student achievement in mathematics: Part 1. Research findings.* Columbus, OH: ERIC Clearinghouse for Science, Mathematics, and Environmental Education. (ERIC Document Reproduction Service No. ED463952)

Hiebert, J., & Carpenter, T. (1992). Learning and teaching with understanding. In D. A. Grouws (Ed.), *Handbook of research on mathematics teaching and learning* (pp. 65–97). New York: Macmillan.

Johnson, D. T. (1993). Mathematics curriculum for the gifted. In J. Van Tassel-Baska (Ed.), *Comprehensive curriculum for gifted learners* (2nd ed., pp. 231–261). Boston: Allyn & Bacon.

LaCelle-Peterson, M., & Rivera, C. (1994). Is it real for all kids? A framework for equitable assessment policies for English language learners. *Harvard Educational Review, 64*(1), 55–75.

Maccini, P., & Hughes, C. A. (2000). Effects of a problem solving strategy on the introductory algebra performance of secondary students with learning disabilities. *Learning Disabilities Research and Practice, 15,* 10–21.

Maker, C. J. (1982). *Curriculum development for the gifted.* Rockville, MD: Aspen.

Mercer, C. D., & Mercer, A. R. (1998). *Teaching students with learning problems* (5th ed.). Upper Saddle River, NJ: Prentice Hall/Merrill.

Montague, M. (1997). Student perception, mathematical problem solving, and learning disabilities. *Remedial and Special Education, 18*(1), 46–53.

National Association for Gifted Children. (2005). *Socio-emotional guidance and counseling: Exploring guiding principle 4.* Retrieved April 23, 2007, from http://www.nagc.org/index.aspx?id=458

National Council of Teachers of Mathematics. (1995). *Assessment standards for school mathematics.* Reston, VA: Author.

National Council of Teachers of Mathematics. (1989). *Curriculum and evaluation standards for school mathematics.* Reston, VA: Author.

National Council of Teachers of Mathematics. (2000). *Principles and standards for school mathematics.* Reston, VA: Author.

National Council of Teachers of Mathematics. (2001). *Mathematics assessment: A practical handbook for grades 3–5.* Reston, VA: Author.

National Council of Teachers of Mathematics. (2006). *Curriculum focal points for prekindergarten through grade 8 mathematics: A quest for coherence.* Retrieved May 13, 2007, from http://nctm.org/focalpoints/

National Council of Teachers of Mathematics. (2007). *Classic middle-grades problems for the classroom, 2000–2007.* Retrieved April 29, 2007, from the National Council of Teachers of Mathematics Web site: http://illuminations.nctm.org/LessonDetail.aspx?id=L264

Neuschwander, C. (1998). *Amanda Bean's amazing dream.* New York: Scholastic Press.

Phillips, E. (1991). *Curriculum and evaluation standards for school mathematics, addenda series, grades 5–8: Patterns and functions.* Reston, VA: National Council of Teachers of Mathematics.

Pintrich, P. R., & Schrauben, B. (1992). Students' motivational beliefs and their cognitive engagement in classroom academic tasks. In D. H. Schunk & J. Meece (Eds.), *Student perceptions in the classroom* (pp. 149–179). Hillsdale, NJ: Lawrence Erlbaum.

Polya, G. (1945). *How to solve it!* Garden City, NY: Doubleday.

Pugalee, D. K. (1997). Connecting writing to the mathematics curriculum. *Mathematics Teacher, 90*(4), 308–310.

Roddick, C. & Bergthold, T. A. (2004). Sixth grade mathematics teachers in transition: A case study. In D. E. McDougall and J. A. Ross (Eds.), *Proceedings of the annual meeting of the North American chapter of the International Group for the Psychology of Mathematics Education (26th, Toronto, Ontario, Canada, October 21–24, 2004), 3,* 1021–1028.

Sierpinska, A. (1998). Three epistemologies, three views of classroom communication: Constructivism, sociocultural approaches, interactionism. In H. Steinbring, M. Bussi, & A. Sierpinska (Eds.), *Language and communication in the mathematics classroom* (pp. 30–62). Reston, VA: National Council of Teachers of Mathematics.

Sliva, J. A. (2003). *Teaching inclusive mathematics to special learners, K–6.* Thousand Oaks, CA: Corwin Press.

Sliva, J. A., & Roddick, C. (2001). Mathematics autobiographies: A window into beliefs, values, and past mathematics experiences of preservice teachers. *Academic Education Quarterly, 5*(2), 101–107.

Tuscon Unified School District Balanced Literacy Booklets, High School. (n.d.). *Best practices in teaching mathematics.* Retrieved April 23, 2007, from http://instech.tusd.k12.az.us/balancedlit/handbook/BLHS/blmathhs.htm

Wiggins, G., & McTighe, J. (1998). *Understanding by design.* Alexandria, VA: Association for Supervision and Curriculum Development.

Index

CORWIN PRESS

The Corwin Press logo—a raven striding across an open book—represents the union of courage and learning. Corwin Press is committed to improving education for all learners by publishing books and other professional development resources for those serving the field of PreK–12 education. By providing practical, hands-on materials, Corwin Press continues to carry out the promise of its motto: **"Helping Educators Do Their Work Better."**

Lightning Source UK Ltd.
Milton Keynes UK
UKHW030730220120
357400UK00005B/67